101 *Quick and Easy*

BlenderBottle®

RECIPES

ISBN 978-0-615-31586-7

Welcome to the BlenderBottle Recipe Book

Whether you've just purchased your first BlenderBottle or you're a seasoned mixing veteran, you are about to discover 101 ways the BlenderBottle can make your life easier.

The BlenderBottle is perfect for mixing the tastiest lump-free drinks with ease. Protein shakes, health supplements, and on-the-go smoothies whip up incredibly smooth every time. What many people don't realize, however, is that the BlenderBottle can mix so much more!

This BlenderBottle Recipe Book sports recipes for everything from delicious twists on protein shakes to savory steak marinades. Each recipe utilizes the power and convenience of the BlenderBottle in order to simplify your life. Whether you're whipping up a 30-second fruit smoothie or preparing a multi-course dinner for a family gathering, the BlenderBottle will make light work of your mixing needs.

Before you begin, we recommend you take a moment to check out the Usage & Tips section that follows—it contains valuable insights from our BlenderBottle experts. The BlenderBottle is designed to make your life easier, and we hope this recipe book fulfills the same purpose. If you have questions, comments, or concerns, feel free to contact us at **www.blenderbottle.com.** Enjoy!

Sincerely,
The BlenderBottle Team

Using Your BlenderBottle

The BlenderBottle is fast, simple, and effective. To use, simply drop the BlenderBall® wire whisk into the BlenderBottle along with your ingredients, screw on the lid, press down the flip top, and shake! The patented BlenderBall moves freely throughout the bottle as you shake, mixing even the thickest ingredients with ease. The BlenderBall is made of 316 surgical-grade stainless steel (so it won't rust, chip, or peel) and is designed to remain in the cup until you've enjoyed the contents.

Color-Coding System

This BlenderBottle Recipe Book features a unique color-coding system that allows you to quickly see which ingredients to mix in the BlenderBottle. For example, in the "Peach Cobbler" recipe shown below, you'll notice three of the ingredients are marked with blue arrows. Simply toss those ingredients into the BlenderBottle and continue with the rest of the recipe. This way you won't accidentally add butter to the BlenderBottle that is supposed to be melted in the baking dish!

Peach Cobbler

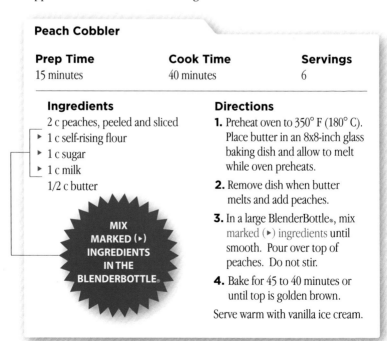

Prep Time	Cook Time	Servings
15 minutes	40 minutes	6

Ingredients

2 c peaches, peeled and sliced
▸ 1 c self-rising flour
▸ 1 c sugar
▸ 1 c milk
1/2 c butter

MIX MARKED (▸) INGREDIENTS IN THE BLENDERBOTTLE®

Directions

1. Preheat oven to 350° F (180° C). Place butter in an 8x8-inch glass baking dish and allow to melt while oven preheats.
2. Remove dish when butter melts and add peaches.
3. In a large BlenderBottle®, mix marked (▸) ingredients until smooth. Pour over top of peaches. Do not stir.
4. Bake for 45 to 40 minutes or until top is golden brown.

Serve warm with vanilla ice cream.

Adding Ingredients in the Right Order

Add ingredients to the BlenderBottle in the order listed in the recipe. Adding liquids before dry ingredients prevents stubborn powders from sticking in the bottom of the cup. Trust us on this one.

1  *Add liquids.*

2  *Add dry ingredients and BlenderBall®.*

3  *Shake it up! (See Basic Bottle Shaking below.)*

Basic Bottle Shaking

There are countless ways to shake a BlenderBottle. Once you've mastered the traditional "up and down" motion, the next step is to add a little flick of the wrist. Not only does this look more impressive to those around you, it gets that BlenderBall moving faster. Just need to gently whisk baby formula or a small amount of liquid? Grab the bottle by the lid and swirl the ball around the bottom of the cup.

The BlenderBottle features infinitely variable blending speeds and runs on a 100% natural power source—you! That makes the BlenderBottle both powerful and eco-friendly.

Cleanup

The BlenderBottle and BlenderBall are 100% dishwasher safe. If you prefer, it only takes a few seconds to clean them by hand. Simply add a few drops of soap, fill the bottle about half way with warm water, close the lid, and shake. Rinse the bottle with warm water, and your cleanup is done!

Let's get cooking!

Table of Contents

Appetizers/Side Dishes

Beverages

Mix It Up

Breakfast

Breakfast (Continued)

Omelets

Main Dishes

Salads

Salad Dressings

Marinades and Sauces

Desserts

Desserts (Continued)

Table of Contents

Black Bean and Corn Salsa

Prep Time
10 minutes

Servings
8

Ingredients

1/3 c fresh lime juice
- ▸ 1/2 c olive oil
- ▸ 1 clove garlic, minced
- ▸ 1/8 t ground cayenne pepper
- ▸ 1 t salt

2 (15 oz.) cans black beans, rinsed and drained
1 1/2 c frozen corn kernels
1 avocado, peeled, pitted and diced
1 red bell pepper, chopped
2 tomatoes, chopped
6 green onions, thinly sliced
1/2 c chopped fresh cilantro

Directions

1. In a small BlenderBottle®, combine marked (▸) ingredients and blend until mixed.
2. In a salad bowl, combine remaining ingredients, pour BlenderBottle mixture into bowl, and toss until salad is well-coated.

Serve with corn chips or as a salad.

Tip: *This fresh and mild salsa is great served with blue tortilla chips. It also makes a great stand alone salad!*

Nutritional Information
(per serving: 564 cal., 19.1 g total fat (2.8g sat. fat), 0 mg chol., 303 mg sodium, 278.4 g carbo., 5.2 g sugars, 24.9 g protein)

Cheesy Green Beans

Prep Time	Cook Time	Servings
15 minutes	20 minutes	6

Ingredients

2 (15 oz.) cans French cut green beans
1 1/2 c Swiss cheese, grated
1/2 c cornflake crumbs
- ▸ 1/2 c sour cream
- ▸ 1 T flour
- ▸ 1 t salt
- ▸ 2 t sugar
- ▸ 1 T butter, melted
- ▸ 1/4 c milk
- ▸ 1/8 t ground black pepper
- ▸ 1/8 t onion powder

Directions

1. Preheat oven to 400° F (200° C).
2. Drain green beans and place in a greased 8x8-inch glass baking dish.
3. In a large BlenderBottle®, add marked (▸) ingredients and blend until smooth.
4. Pour BlenderBottle mixture over green beans. Add cheese and mix together. Top with crushed cornflakes.
5. Bake uncovered for 20 minutes.

Nutritional Information

(per serving: 228 cal., 14 g total fat (9g sat. fat), 39 mg chol., 498 mg sodium, 17.3 g carbo., 4.4 g sugars, 11.1 g protein)

Creamy Cucumbers

Prep Time	Servings
15 minutes	6

Ingredients

1 large cucumber, thinly sliced
1/2 small onion, thinly sliced (1/3 cup)
- ▸ 1/2 c sour cream
- ▸ 1 T milk
- ▸ 1 T vinegar
- ▸ 1/2 t salt
- ▸ 1/4 t dried dill
- ▸ Dash black pepper

Directions

1. In a large BlenderBottle®, combine marked (▸) ingredients and mix well.
2. Combine cucumber, onion, and BlenderBottle mixture in a medium nonmetal bowl and toss to coat. Cover and refrigerate for 4 hours or up to 3 days, stirring occasionally. Stir before serving.

Nutritional Information

(per serving: 45 cal., 3 g total fat (2g sat. fat), 7 mg chol., 204 mg sodium, 3 g carbo., 0g sugars, 1 g protein)

Cinnamon-Sugar Pecans

Prep Time
10 minutes

Servings
12

Ingredients

1 pound pecan halves
- ▸ 1 egg white
- ▸ 1 teaspoon ground cinnamon
- ▸ 1 c sugar
- ▸ 3/4 t salt
- ▸ 2 T water

Tip: *Serve as an appetizer, desert, or chop and put on your favorite salad.*

Directions

1. Preheat oven to 250° F (130° C).
2. Spread pecans on lightly buttered baking sheet. Add marked (▸) ingredients to a small BlenderBottle® and shake until well-blended (sugar does not need to dissolve).
3. Pour cinnamon-sugar mixture over pecans and toss until evenly coated. Spread evenly on baking sheet. Bake in preheated oven for 1 hour, stirring every 10-15 minutes.

Nutritional Information

(per serving: 328 cal., 27.2 g total fat (2.3g sat. fat), 0 mg chol., 152 mg sodium, 22.1 g carbo., 18.2 g sugars, 3.8 g protein)

Fantastic Fruit Dip

Prep Time
5 minutes

Makes Approximately
1 1/2 cups

Ingredients

- ▸ 1 1/2 c low-fat vanilla yogurt
- ▸ 4 T powdered sugar
- ▸ 2 T lemon juice
- ▸ 1/4 t cinnamon

Directions

1. In a small BlenderBottle®, combine marked (▸) ingredients and blend until smooth.
2. Pour mixture into serving bowl, cover, and chill in refrigerator for at least 1 hour. Serve with fresh fruit.

Nutritional Information

(per 1/4 cup serving: 61 cal., 1 g total fat (0.6 g sat. fat), 4 mg chol., 43 mg sodium, 10 g carbo., 9 g sugars, 3 g protein)

Potatoes Au Gratin

Prep Time	**Cook Time**	**Servings**
30 minutes	1.5 hours	8

Ingredients

4 russet potatoes, sliced into 1/4 inch slices
1 onion, sliced into rings
4 1/2 T butter
▸ 3 c milk
▸ 4 1/2 T all-purpose flour
▸ 1 t salt
2 1/2 c cheddar cheese, shredded
Salt and pepper

Directions

1. Preheat oven to 400° F (200° C). Grease a 9x13-inch glass casserole dish.
2. In a medium-sized saucepan, melt butter over medium heat. Blend marked (▸) ingredients in a large BlenderBottle® and pour mixture into saucepan.
3. Stir and cook until mixture thickens slightly. Add cheese and continue stirring until melted.
4. Layer half of the potatoes in bottom of casserole dish. Top with onion slices and cover with half of the cheese sauce. Add remaining potatoes and cover with remaining cheese sauce. Salt and pepper to taste.
5. Cover dish with aluminum foil and bake for 1 1/2 hours.

Tip: *For a quicker dish, try substituting frozen hash browns for sliced potatoes. For a crispier top, remove foil for the last 10 minutes of cooking and sprinkle extra cheese on top.*

Nutritional Information

(per serving: 340 cal., 20 g total fat (13g sat. fat), 62 mg chol., 601 mg sodium, 26 g carbo., 6 g sugars, 14 g protein)

Crispy Buffalo Wings

Prep Time	Cook Time	Servings
20 minutes	25 minutes	12

Ingredients

12 chicken wings (about 2 lbs.)
▸ 4 T butter, melted
▸ 6 T hot pepper sauce
▸ 4 t paprika
▸ 1/2 t salt
▸ 1/2 t cayenne pepper
1 recipe Buttermilk Ranch Dressing (pg. 73) or Sweet 'n Tangy Buffalo Wing Dip (pg. 81)

Tip: *Serve with Buttermilk Ranch Dressing (pg. 73) or Sweet N' Tangy Buffalo Wing Dip (pg. 81).*

Directions

1. Cut off and discard tips of chicken wings. Cut wings at joints to make 24 pieces. Place wings in a resealable plastic bag, place in a glass dish, and set aside.
2. In a large BlenderBottle®, combine marked (▸) ingredients and blend until smooth. Pour mixture into bag with chicken wings, seal, and let sit in refrigerator for 30 minutes.
3. When ready to cook, drain marinade and place chicken wings on a large cookie sheet lined with tin foil. Broil 4 to 5 inches from the heat for about 10 minutes or until light brown. Turn wings. Broil for an additional 10 to 15 minutes or until chicken is tender and no longer pink inside.

Nutritional Information
(per serving: 181 cal., 9.6 g total fat (4g sat. fat), 77 mg chol., 235 mg sodium, 0.5 g carbo., 0g sugars, 22 g protein)

Grilled Veggies

Prep Time	Cook Time	Servings
15 minutes	15 minutes	4

Ingredients

1/2 c zucchini, thickly sliced
1/2 c red bell pepper, sliced
1/2 c yellow bell pepper, sliced
1/2 c yellow squash, sliced
1/2 c red onion, sliced
1 c mushrooms, sliced
16 cherry tomatoes
▸ 1/4 c olive oil
▸ 1/2 c soy sauce
▸ 1/2 c lemon juice
▸ 1 clove garlic, crushed

Directions

1. Place all vegetables in a large glass bowl.
2. Blend marked (▸) ingredients in a small BlenderBottle® and pour over vegetables.
3. Cover bowl and let marinate in the refrigerator for 30 minutes.
4. Cook vegetables directly on grill or on skewers over medium heat. Turn every 2 to 3 minutes per side or to desired doneness.

Tip: *Goes well with Key West Chicken (pg. 55) or any other favorite grilled main course.*

Nutritional Information
(per serving: 255 cal., 14.7 g total fat (2 g sat. fat), 0 mg chol., 1828 mg sodium, 28 g carbo., 16 g sugars, 8 g protein)

Lemon Ginger Fruit Dip

Prep Time
10 minutes

Makes Approximately
2 cups

Ingredients

- ▸ 1 c plain yogurt
- ▸ 1 c sour cream
- ▸ 2 T honey
- ▸ 3/4 t ginger
- ▸ 1/2 t lemon juice
- ▸ Grated lemon zest

Directions

1. In a small BlenderBottle®, combine marked (▸) ingredients and blend until smooth.
2. Pour mixture into serving bowl, cover, and chill in refrigerator for at least 1 hour before serving. Serve with fresh fruit.

Nutritional Information
(per 1/4 cup serving: 97 cal., 6.5 g total fat (4.1 g sat. fat), 14 mg chol., 37 mg sodium, 8 g carbo., 6.5 g sugars, 3 g protein)

Yorkshire Pudding

Prep Time:
20 minutes

Servings:
6

Ingredients:

- ▸ 3 eggs
- ▸ 3/4 c milk
- ▸ 1/2 t salt
- ▸ 3/4 c all-purpose flour
- 1/2 c pan drippings from roast beef*

***Note:** *If you do not have pan drippings, you can substitute thickened beef or vegetable broth, Worcestershire sauce with butter or oil, or omit the drippings altogether.*

Directions:

1. Preheat oven to 450° F (230° C).
2. In a large BlenderBottle®, combine marked (▸) ingredients and blend until smooth.
3. Pour drippings into a 9-inch pie pan, cast iron skillet, or square baking dish. Put pan in oven and heat drippings until smoking hot. Carefully remove pan from oven and add BlenderBottle mixture. Put pan back in oven and cook until puffed and dry (about 15 to 20 minutes).

Nutritional Information
(per serving: 107 cal., 3 g total fat (1.1g sat. fat), 96 mg chol., 301 mg sodium, 13.6 g carbo., 1.8 g sugars, 5.8 g protein)

Tangy Meatball Bites

Prep Time	Cook Time	Servings
15 minutes	25 minutes	4

Ingredients

- 1 lb. ground beef
- 1 egg
- 1/2 c saltine crackers, crushed
- 2 T milk
- 1/2 t rubbed sage
- ▸ 1/2 c water
- ▸ 1/4 c ketchup
- ▸ 2 T brown sugar
- ▸ 1 T soy sauce
- ▸ 1 T vinegar

Directions:

1. In a medium bowl, combine ground beef, egg, crackers, milk, and sage. Mix well and shape into 1-inch balls.
2. In a large skillet, brown meatballs over medium heat; drain.
3. In a small BlenderBottle®, mix marked (▸) ingredients. Pour over meatballs and bring to a boil. Reduce heat and cover for 15-20 minutes or until meatball centers are no longer pink and thoroughly cooked.

Nutritional Information

(per serving: 289 cal., 9 g total fat (3.3g sat. fat), 148 mg chol., 549 mg sodium, 13 g carbo., 8.4 g sugars, 37 g protein)

Zesty Marinated Shrimp Bowl

Prep Time:
25 minutes

Servings:
10

Ingredients:

5 lbs. frozen, cooked shrimp
- ▸ 1/2 c olive oil
- ▸ 1/2 c white or red wine vinegar
- ▸ 1 1/2 t lemon peel, finely shredded
- ▸ 1/4 c lemon juice
- ▸ 2 T tomato paste
- ▸ 1 T honey
- ▸ 3 cloves garlic, minced
- ▸ 2 t fresh ginger, grated (or 1/8 t dried)
- ▸ 1/2 t salt
- ▸ 1/4 t cayenne pepper

Directions:

1. Place shrimp in large strainer and rinse with cold water until thawed.
2. Arrange shrimp in circular layers in a glass bowl approximately 7 to 8 inches in diameter and about 4 inches deep Arrange with tails in center and round shrimp backs facing out. Continue adding layers until bowl is filled. Press down on shrimp with bottom of plate to compress layers as needed.
3. In a small BlenderBottle®, combine marked (▸) ingredients and shake until well-mixed. Pour marinade over shrimp, cover, and chill in refrigerator overnight.
4. When ready to serve, place a large plate slightly off-center over the bowl and invert to drain marinade. Place a platter with 1/2 inch sides over bowl, carefully invert, and slowly remove bowl to leave shrimp in molded shape.

Nutritional Information
(per serving: 336 cal., 13 g total fat (2.2g sat. fat), 442 mg chol., 629 mg sodium, 3.6 g carbo., 2.4 g sugars, 47.7 g protein)

101 Flavors Yogurt Smoothie

Prep Time
3 minutes

Servings
1

Ingredients

- ▸ 1 c milk
- ▸ 1 c yogurt (any flavor)
- ▸ 1 serving vanilla protein powder

Directions

1. Combine marked (▸) ingredients in a large BlenderBottle® and shake until smooth.

***Note:** *Substitute your favorite yogurt flavor for delicious smoothie variations.*

Nutritional Information
(per serving: 396 cal., 10.6 g total fat (6.5 g sat. fat), 84 mg chol., 392 mg sodium, 32.7 g carbo., 32.6 g sugars, 42 g protein)

Cinnamon Roll Protein Shake

Prep Time
5 minutes

Servings
1

Ingredients

- ▸ 8 oz. low fat milk
- ▸ 1 serving vanilla protein powder
- ▸ 1 T instant vanilla pudding (sugar free or regular)
- ▸ 1/4 t cinnamon
- ▸ 1/4 t vanilla extract
- ▸ Few dashes butter flavored powder or extract

Directions

1. Place marked (▸) ingredients in a large BlenderBottle® and shake until smooth.

Nutritional Information
(per serving: 220 cal., 4.2 g total fat (2.4 g sat. fat), 61 mg chol., 220 mg sodium, 15.9 g carbo., 20 g sugars, 28.7 g protein)

Easy as Apple Pie Shake

Prep Time
5 minutes

Servings
1

Ingredients

- ▸ 1 c milk
- ▸ 1/2 c plain yogurt
- ▸ 1/2 c unsweetened applesauce
- ▸ Pinch of cinnamon (to taste)
- ▸ Pinch of nutmeg (optional)
- ▸ 1 serving vanilla protein powder

Directions

1. Place marked (▸) ingredients in a large BlenderBottle® and shake until smooth.

Nutritional Information

(per serving: 374 cal., 8.9 g total fat (5.4 g sat. fat), 77 mg chol., 308 mg sodium, 38.2 g carbo., 36.4 g sugars, 35.7 g protein)

Classic BlenderBottle® Smoothie

Prep Time
3 minutes

Servings
1

Ingredients

- ▸ 1 c raspberry yogurt, seedless*
- ▸ 1/2 c cranberry juice*
- ▸ 1/2 c milk
- ▸ 1 serving vanilla protein powder

Directions

1. Place marked (▸) ingredients in a BlenderBottle and shake until smooth.

***Note:** *Substitute your favorite yogurt and juice flavors to create your own unique blend!*

Nutritional Information

(per serving: 357 cal., 8.3 g total fat (5 g sat. fat), 342 mg chol., 342 mg sodium, 32.8 g carbo., 28.3 g sugars, 38.1 g protein)

Orange Dream Shake

Prep Time:
5 minutes

Servings:
1

Ingredients:
- ▸ 1 c orange juice, pulp free
- ▸ 1 c vanilla ice cream, softened

Directions:
1. Combine marked (▸) ingredients in a BlenderBottle® and shake until smooth.

Nutritional Information
(per serving: 401 cal., 16.3 g total fat (9.8 g sat. fat), 63 mg chol., 118 mg sodium, 59.8 g carbo., 51.4 g sugars, 6.8 g protein)

Iced Cocoa/Coffee

Prep Time
5 minutes

Servings
1

Ingredients
- ▸ 1 c hot cocoa or brewed coffee, cooled
- ▸ 1/2 c crushed ice
- ▸ 1 T coffee creamer
- ▸ 1 packet of Stevia (optional)

Directions
1. Combine marked (▸) ingredients in a large BlenderBottle® and shake until smooth.

Tip: *Try adding one serving of vanilla protein powder for added nutrition!*

Nutritional Information
(per serving: 32 cal., 2.9 g total fat (1.8 g sat. fat), 10 mg chol., 14 mg sodium, 0.6 g carbo., 0 g sugars, 0.7 g protein)

"On the Run" Fruit Shake

Prep Time
5 minutes

Servings
1

Ingredients

- ▸ 6-8 oz. fruit juice (any flavor)
- ▸ 1 scoop vanilla protein powder

Directions

1. Blend marked (▸) ingredients in a small BlenderBottle® until smooth.

Nutritional Information

(per serving: 200 cal., 2.2 g total fat (1 g sat. fat), 50 mg chol., 125 mg sodium, 24 g carbo., 21.5 g sugars, 21 g protein)

Peanut Brittle Protein Shake

Prep Time
5 minutes

Servings
1

Ingredients

- ▸ 8 oz. low fat milk
- ▸ 2 T instant sugar-free butterscotch pudding mix (dry)
- ▸ 1 serving vanilla protein powder
- ▸ 1 T peanut butter (smooth)

Directions

1. Combine marked (▸) ingredients in a large BlenderBottle® and shake until smooth.

Tip: *Try using chunky peanut butter to make this shake chunky like real peanut brittle!*

Nutritional Information

(per serving: 240 cal., 10 g total fat (2.5 g sat. fat), 50 mg chol., 123 mg sodium, 7 g carbo., 10 g sugars, 26 g protein)

Peanut Butter Cup Protein Shake

Prep Time
5 minutes

Servings
1

Ingredients

- ▸ 8 oz. low fat milk
- ▸ 1 T natural peanut butter, smooth
- ▸ 1 serving chocolate protein powder*

***Note:** *You can substitute vanilla protein powder plus 1 T cocoa powder.*

Directions

1. In order listed, place marked (▸) ingredients in a large BlenderBottle® and mix until smooth.

Nutritional Information

(per serving: 315 cal., 12.2 g total fat (3.9 g sat. fat), 61 mg chol., 223 mg sodium, 18.3 g carbo., 16 g sugars, 33.6 g protein)

Pomegranate Lemonade

Prep Time
5 minutes

Servings
2

Ingredients

- ▸ 1 1/2 c water
- ▸ 1/3 c white sugar
- ▸ 1/3 c lemon juice
- ▸ 3 T pomegranate juice

Directions

1. Mix marked (▸) ingredients in a large BlenderBottle®. Serve over ice.

Tip: *Try substituting agave nectar for the sugar for a lower glycemic alternative.*

Nutritional Information

(per serving: 150 cal., 0 g total fat (0 g sat. fat), 0 mg chol., 6 mg sodium, 40 g carbo., 36 g sugars, 0.2 g protein)

Piña Colada Escape

Prep Time
3 minutes

Servings
1

Ingredients

- ▸ 1/2 c pineapple juice
- ▸ 1 (8 oz.) piña colada yogurt
- ▸ 1/2 c milk (optional)
- ▸ 1 serving vanilla protein powder (optional)

Directions

1. Combine marked (▸) ingredients in a large BlenderBottle® and shake until smooth.

Nutritional Information

(per serving (with protein powder): 390 cal., 8.1 g total fat (4.8 g sat. fat), 73 mg chol., 331 mg sodium, 41.8 g carbo., 37.6 g sugars, 37.4 g protein)

Triple Juice Punch

Prep Time
5 minutes

Servings
1

Ingredients

- ▸ 1 c pineapple juice
- ▸ 1 c orange juice
- ▸ 1 1/2 T fresh squeezed lemon juice

Directions

1. Combine marked (▸) ingredients in a large BlenderBottle® and shake until mixed.

Nutritional Information

(per serving: 250 cal., 0.8 g total fat (0 g sat. fat), 0 mg chol., 8 mg sodium, 59.9 g carbo., 46.3 g sugars, 2.7 g protein)

Mix it Up!

Add a little variety to your every-day shakes!
Try adding one or more of these ingredients to your protein or nutrition shake and enjoy a new treat every day!

- ☐ Ground oatmeal
- ☐ Cocoa powder
- ☐ Cinnamon
- ☐ Peanut butter
- ☐ Yogurt
- ☐ Fruit juice (fresh or frozen concentrate)
- ☐ Softened ice cream
- ☐ Cake mix
- ☐ Extract (e.g. vanilla, almond, peppermint, etc.)
- ☐ Fruit preserves
- ☐ Applesauce
- ☐ Instant pudding mix (e.g. pistachio, butterscotch, banana, etc.)
- ☐ Soy or rice milk
- ☐ Whipping cream
- ☐ Almond butter
- ☐ Flavored syrup (chocolate, strawberry, butterscotch, etc.)
- ☐ Agave nectar
- ☐ Maple syrup
- ☐ Malted milk powder
- ☐ Nutella
- ☐ Coconut milk
- ☐ Finely crushed cookies (e.g. Oreos, graham crackers, etc.)
- ☐ Flavored hot cocoa mix (raspberry, mint, hazelnut, etc.)
- ☐ Apple cider mix

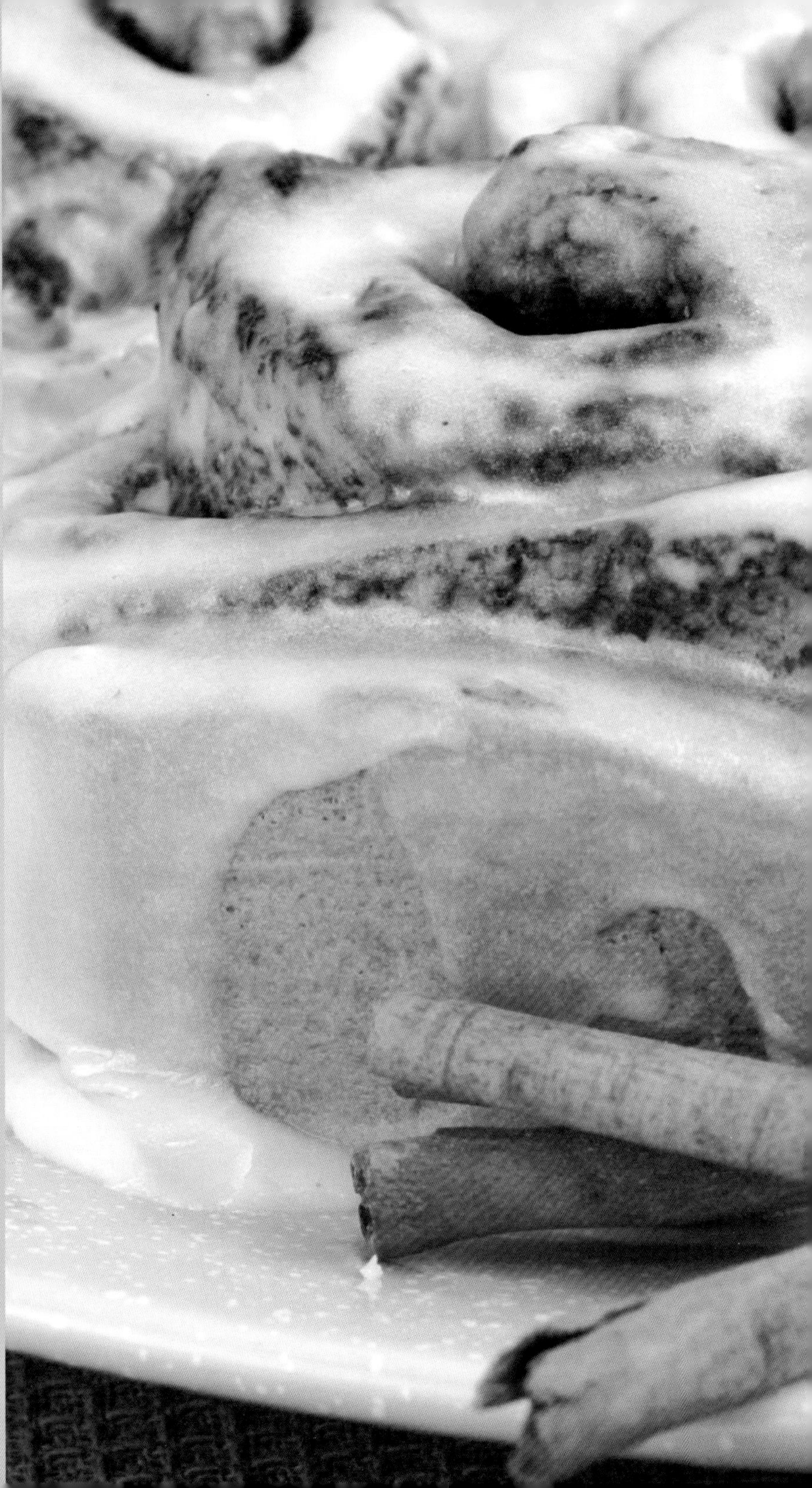

Blend N' Bake Sticky Buns

Prep Time	Cook Time	Servings
10 minutes	30 minutes	12

Ingredients

1 package frozen bake n' serve dinner rolls (24 rolls)

- ▸ 1 (3.5 oz.) package butterscotch cook n' serve pudding
- ▸ 1 t cinnamon
- ▸ 1 c brown sugar

Directions

1. Thoroughly grease or butter Bundt pan and place frozen rolls on bottom.
2. Place marked (▸) ingredients in a small BlenderBottle® and shake until mixed. Sprinkle dry mixture over top of rolls.
3. Cover loosely with foil and let stand at room temperature overnight.
4. The following morning, bake rolls at 350° F (180° C) for 30 minutes or until golden brown. Remove from oven and carefully turn upside down on a large plate. Serve warm.

Nutritional Information

(per serving: 612 cal., 11.1 g total fat (2.4 g sat. fat), 7 mg chol., 1005 mg sodium, 109.5 g carbo., 27.8 g sugars, 18.7 g protein)

BlenderBottle® Crepes

Prep Time	Cook Time	Chill Time	Servings
5 minutes	10 minutes	20 minutes	4

Ingredients

- ▸ 3 eggs
- ▸ 3/4 c and 2 T milk
- ▸ 3 T flour
- ▸ 1 T sugar
- ▸ 1 pinch of salt

Directions

1. Combine marked (▸) ingredients in a large BlenderBottle and shake until smooth. Let sit in refrigerator for 20 minutes.
2. Heat a large, lightly greased pan over medium heat. Pour approximately 1/4 cup of batter onto pan and tilt pan with a circular motion to evenly coat surface.
3. Cook for 1-2 minutes, until the bottom is slightly brown. Carefully flip crepe and cook other side.
4. Fill with fruit and yogurt, ham and cheese, ice cream and berries, or your favorite crepe filling.

Nutritional Information
(per serving: 107 cal., 4.4 g total fat (1.7 g sat. fat), 144 mg chol., 107 mg sodium, 10.4 g carbo., 6 g sugars, 6.5 g protein)

BlenderBottle® Pancakes

Prep Time	Cook Time	Servings
5 minutes	10 minutes	4

Ingredients

- ▸ 1 1/3 c milk
- ▸ 1 1/4 c flour
- ▸ 2 T sugar
- ▸ 3 T vegetable oil
- ▸ 1 egg
- ▸ 3/4 t salt
- ▸ 2 t baking powder

Directions

1. Preheat a griddle or large skillet and lightly grease.
2. Combine marked (▸) ingredients in a large BlenderBottle and blend until mixed. (Note: baking powder will create minor pressure inside the BlenderBottle. Open carefully.)
3. Pour batter onto griddle or skillet and cook until golden, flipping once.

Serve with maple syrup or fresh fruit and whipped cream.

Nutritional Information

(per serving: 316 cal., 13.3 g total fat (3.4 g sat. fat), 53 mg chol., 490 mg sodium, 41 g carbo., 10 g sugars, 8 g protein)

BlenderBottle® Waffles

Prep Time	Cook Time	Servings
5 minutes	15 minutes	4

Ingredients

- ▸ 1 c milk
- ▸ 1 1/4 c all-purpose flour
- ▸ 1/4 t salt
- ▸ 3 t granulated sugar
- ▸ 2 eggs
- ▸ 1/4 c vegetable oil
- ▸ 1/4 t pure vanilla extract
- ▸ 1 t baking powder

Directions

1. Spray waffle iron with cooking spray and preheat.
2. Mix marked (▸) ingredients in a large BlenderBottle and shake until combined. (Note: baking powder will create minor pressure inside the BlenderBottle. Open carefully.)
3. Pour batter onto waffle iron and cook until golden brown.

Serve warm with syrup or fresh fruit and whipped cream.

Nutritional Information

(per serving: 339 cal., 17.4 g total fat (4.2 g sat. fat), 98 mg chol., 205 mg sodium, 37 g carbo., 6.5 g sugars, 8.8 g protein)

Pumpkin Pancakes

Prep Time	Cook Time	Servings
10 minutes	10 minutes	3

Ingredients

- ▸ 1 T vinegar
- ▸ 1 T vegetable oil
- ▸ 1 egg
- ▸ 1/2 c pumpkin puree
- ▸ 3/4 c milk
- ▸ 1/4 t salt
- ▸ 1/4 t ground ginger
- ▸ 1/2 t ground cinnamon
- ▸ 1/2 t ground allspice
- ▸ 1/2 t baking soda
- ▸ 1 t baking powder
- ▸ 2 1/2 T brown sugar
- ▸ 1 c all-purpose flour

Directions

1. Preheat lightly greased pancake griddle or pan.
2. Combine marked (▸) ingredients in a large BlenderBottle® and blend just until mixed. Do not over-mix. (Note: baking powder will create pressure inside the BlenderBottle. Open carefully.)
3. Pour approximately 1/4 cup of batter onto preheated griddle and cook until golden, flipping once.

Top with butter and warm maple syrup.

Nutritional Information

(per serving: 291 cal., 7.8 g total fat (2.2 g sat. fat), 67 mg chol., 457 mg sodium, 50 g carbo., 12 g sugars, 9 g protein)

German Pancakes

Prep Time	Cook Time	Servings
5 minutes	15 minutes	4

Ingredients

1 T butter, melted
- ▸ 3 eggs
- ▸ 1/2 c milk
- ▸ 1/2 c flour
- ▸ Dash salt

Directions

1. Preheat oven to 425° F (220° C). Place butter in a 9x9-inch pan and place in preheating oven to melt.
2. In a large BlenderBottle®, mix marked (▸) ingredients until well blended. Pour BlenderBottle mixture into buttered pan and bake for 12-15 minutes or until golden brown. Top with lemon juice and powdered sugar, berries and whipped cream, or warm syrup.

Tip: *Delicious served warm with lemon juice, berries, and powdered sugar.*

Nutritional Information
(per serving: 145 cal., 6.9 g total fat (3.2 g sat. fat), 150 mg chol., 118 mg sodium, 13.6 g carbo., 1.8 g sugars, 6.8 g protein)

Fast Frittata

Prep Time	Cook Time	Servings
15 minutes	30 minutes	6

Ingredients

- ▸ 6 eggs
- ▸ 1 c milk
- ▸ 1/2 t salt
- ▸ 1/2 t dried oregano
- ▸ Black pepper to taste
- 4 oz. sliced mushrooms
- 3-5 green onions, chopped
- 10 slices pre-cooked bacon
- 1 c cheddar cheese, shredded

Tip: *Try substituting the last four ingredients with almost any veggies, cheeses, and meats you happen to have around.*

Directions

1. Preheat oven to 350° F (180° C) and coat an 8x8-inch glass baking dish with cooking spray.
2. In a large BlenderBottle®, blend marked (▸) ingredients and pour into baking dish.
3. Sprinkle egg mixture with mushrooms, green onions, and bacon. Top with cheese.
4. Bake uncovered for 30-35 minutes or until a knife inserted in the center comes out clean.

Serve warm and, if desired, with tomato sauce or salsa.

Nutritional Information

(per serving: 422 cal., 31 g total fat (12 g sat. fat), 261 mg chol., 1483 mg sodium, 4.4 g carbo., 3 g sugars, 30 g protein)

BlenderBottle® Classic French Toast

Prep Time	Cook Time	Servings
10 minutes	10 minutes	5

Ingredients

10 thick slices of bread
- ▸ 1 c milk
- ▸ 1/4 c all-purpose flour
- ▸ 3 eggs
- ▸ 1 T white sugar
- ▸ 1 t vanilla extract
- ▸ 1/2 t ground cinnamon
- ▸ 1 pinch salt

Directions

1. In a large BlenderBottle, mix marked (▸) ingredients until well blended. Pour mixture into shallow pie tin or bowl.
2. Heat a lightly oiled griddle or frying pan over medium heat.
3. Soak bread slices in mixture until saturated. Cook each slice on griddle or frying pan until golden brown on both sides. Serve hot.

Nutritional Information

(per serving: 146 cal., 4.2 g total fat (1.6 g sat. fat), 116 mg chol., 211 mg sodium, 19.2 g carbo., 6.1 g sugars, 7 g protein)

Peaches and Cream French Toast

Prep Time	Cook Time	Servings
10 minutes	30 minutes	4

Ingredients

1/2 loaf French bread, sliced
- ▸ 6 eggs
- ▸ 2 c half and half or light whipping cream
- ▸ 4 T peach preserves

Directions

1. Arrange sliced bread in bottom of lightly greased 8x8-inch glass baking dish.
2. Blend marked (▸) ingredients in a large BlenderBottle® and pour over bread.
3. Refrigerate for at least 1 hour, then bake for 30 minutes at 350° F (180° C).

Dust with powdered sugar and top with peaches and/or maple syrup.

Nutritional Information

(per serving: 492 cal., 21 g total fat (11 g sat. fat), 324 mg chol., 564 mg sodium, 55 g carbo., 12 g sugars, 20 g protein)

Macadamia Nut French Toast

Prep Time	Cook Time	Servings
15 minutes	30 minutes	6

Ingredients

- ▸ 4 eggs
- ▸ 2/3 c orange juice
- ▸ 1/3 c milk
- ▸ 1/4 c sugar
- ▸ 1 tsp vanilla
- 1 loaf French bread, cut into 1 1/2 inch slices
- 1/3 c butter, melted
- 1/4 c sliced macadamia nuts

Directions

1. Lightly grease a 9x13-inch baking dish with cooking spray. Arrange a single layer of bread in the bottom of the dish.
2. In a large BlenderBottle®, combine marked (▸) ingredients and blend until smooth. Pour egg mixture over bread. Cover and refrigerate at least one hour, turning once.
3. Preheat oven to 400° F (200° C). Pour melted butter over bread. Sprinkle with macadamia nuts and bake for 25-30 minutes or until bread is puffy and golden brown.

Serve with butter and warm syrup.

Note: *If using a dark non-stick pan, reduce baking temperature to 350° F (180° C).*

Nutritional Information

(per serving: 472 cal., 19 g total fat (8.7 g sat. fat), 152 mg chol., 675 mg sodium, 61 g carbo., 14 g sugars, 15 g protein)

Raspberry Cream Cheese French Toast

Prep Time	Cook Time	Servings
15 minutes + at least 1 hour refrigeration	30 minutes	4

Ingredients

6-8 slices wholegrain bread
8-10 oz. fresh or frozen raspberries
4 oz. cream cheese
▸ 3/4 c milk
▸ 4 large eggs
▸ 1 t cinnamon
▸ 1 t vanilla extract
Powdered sugar

Topping

1/8 c butter, softened
1/4 c brown sugar
1 T pure maple syrup

Directions

1. Lightly grease an 8x8-inch baking dish and place one layer of sliced bread on bottom (3-4 slices depending on size).
2. Layer raspberries over bread.
3. Spread cream cheese on 3-4 additional slices of bread and place, cream cheese side down, on top of raspberries.
4. In a large BlenderBottle®, mix marked (▸) ingredients and pour over bread, allowing mixture to soak into bread.
5. Cover and refrigerate at least one hour (or overnight).

After soaking

1. Preheat oven to 350° F (180° C).
2. Mix Topping ingredients and spread on French toast.
3. Bake for about 30 minutes or until top is slightly brown and crisp.

Dust with powdered sugar. Serve with maple syrup or yogurt.

Nutritional Information

(per serving: 493 cal., 23 g total fat (12.4 g sat. fat), 262 mg chol., 482 mg sodium, 54 g carbo., 30 g sugars, 18 g protein)

BlenderBottle® Classic Omelet

Prep Time	Cook Time	Servings
5 minutes	5 minutes	1

Ingredients

1 T butter or oil
▸ 2 large eggs
▸ Salt and pepper to taste

Fillings of your choice.

Some suggestions include:

- Tomatoes, diced
- Cheese, shredded
- Peppers, diced
- Ham, diced
- Bacon, chopped
- Scallions, chopped
- Avocado, diced
- Salsa

Directions

1. Whip marked (▸) ingredients in a BlenderBottle® until frothy.
2. Heat butter or oil in 9-inch non-stick frying pan. Pour in egg mixture.
3. After about 15 seconds, use spatula to cut 6-8 small cuts through omelet (to allow uncooked egg to flow to bottom of pan).
4. When top is nearly set, sprinkle fillings over half of omelet and turn off heat. When egg is cooked, fold omelet in half with spatula.
Serve warm.

Nutritional Information

(per serving (plain omelet with 1/2 c cheddar cheese): 473 cal., 40 g total fat (22.3 g sat. fat), 513 mg chol., 573 mg sodium, 1.6 g carbo., 1.1 g sugars, 26.8 g protein)

French Egg-White Omelet

Prep Time	Cook Time	Servings
5 minutes	10 minutes	2

Ingredients

1 t olive oil
- ▸ 6 egg whites
- ▸ 1 T water
- ▸ 1 t salt
- ▸ 1/2 t black pepper

Fillings of your choice

Some suggestions include:

- Tomatoes, diced
- Cheese, shredded
- Peppers, diced
- Ham, diced
- Bacon, chopped
- Scallions, chopped
- Avocado, diced
- Salsa

Directions

1. Heat oil in omelet pan on high heat.
2. Combine marked (▸) ingredients in a large BlenderBottle® and whip until smooth and frothy.
3. Pour mixture into pan and cook over medium-high heat until slightly brown. Add your favorite fillings to center and fold over. Serve warm.

Nutritional Information

(per serving (plain omelet with 1/2 c cheddar cheese): 183 cal., 11.8 g total fat (6.3 g sat. fat), 30 mg chol., 1503 mg sodium, 1.4 g carbo., 0.8 g sugars, 17.9 g protein)

Oven Omelet

Prep Time	Cook Time	Servings
10 minutes	50 minutes	6

Ingredients

2 c shredded hash browns*

1 c diced cooked ham

1 c sharp cheddar cheese, shredded

- ▸ 8 eggs
- ▸ 1 c milk
- ▸ Salt and pepper to taste

Directions

1. Preheat oven to 350° F (180° C). Place hash browns in lightly greased 8x8-inch glass baking dish. Layer ham and cheese on top of hash browns.
2. In a large BlenderBottle®, mix together marked (▸) ingredients until smooth. Pour egg mixture evenly over ingredients in baking dish.
3. Bake in preheated oven for 45-50 minutes, or until knife inserted in middle comes out clean. Serve warm. Goes great with salsa!

***Tip:** *For a quick variation, try using frozen O'Brian-style hash browns (potatoes with chopped peppers and onions).*

Nutritional Information

(per serving: 107 cal., 4.4 g total fat (1.7 g sat. fat), 144 mg chol., 107 mg sodium, 10.4 g carbo., 6 g sugars, 6.5 g protein)

Asian Salmon

Prep Time	Prep Time	Servings
15 minutes	30 minutes	6

Ingredients

2 lbs. salmon fillets, with skin
- ▸ 2 T olive oil
- ▸ 2 T rice vinegar
- ▸ 2 T soy sauce
- ▸ 2 T onion, minced
- ▸ 2 cloves garlic, minced
- ▸ 1 T packed brown sugar
- ▸ 1 T sesame oil
- ▸ 1 pinch ground black pepper

Directions

1. Make several shallow slashes in the skinless side of the salmon fillets. Place skin-side down in a 9x13-inch glass baking dish.
2. Combine marked (▸) ingredients in a small BlenderBottle®, blend well, and pour over salmon. Cover and refrigerate for 1 to 2 hours.
3. Preheat oven to 350° F (180° C). Remove cover from salmon and bake in the marinating dish for about 30 minutes or until fish is cooked and can be flaked with a fork.

Tip: *Great served over rice with a side of grilled vegetables (pg. 20).*

Nutritional Information

(per serving: 386 cal., 25.5 g total fat (4.7 g sat. fat), 95 mg chol., 394 mg sodium, 2.5 g carbo., 1.7 g sugars, 33.9 g protein)

Barbecue Beef

Prep Time	Cook Time	Servings
10 minutes	8-10 hours (in slow cooker)	8

Ingredients

- ▸ 1 1/2 c ketchup
- ▸ 1/4 c packed brown sugar
- ▸ 1/4 c red wine vinegar
- ▸ 2 T prepared Dijon-style mustard
- ▸ 3 T Worcestershire sauce
- ▸ 1 t liquid smoke flavoring
- ▸ 1/2 t salt
- ▸ 1/2 t ground black pepper
- ▸ 1/4 t garlic powder
- 1 (2.5-4 lb) boneless chuck roast

Directions

1. Place marked (▸) ingredients in a small BlenderBottle® and mix until smooth.
2. Place roast in a slow cooker and pour BlenderBottle mixture over it. Cover and cook on low for approximately 8-10 hours.
3. Remove roast from slow cooker, shred with a fork (remove any fat), and return to slow cooker. Stir meat to evenly coat with sauce. Continue cooking approximately 1 hour or until done.

Serve over rice, potatoes, or in sandwich buns.

Nutritional Information

(per serving: 636 cal., 40.8 g total fat (16 g sat. fat), 168 mg chol., 868 mg sodium, 17.3 g carbo., 15.9 g sugars, 47.6 g protein)

BlenderBottle® Bourbon Chicken

Prep Time	Cook Time	Servings
20 minutes	25 minutes	6

Ingredients

2 lbs. boneless chicken breasts, cut into bite-size pieces
1 1/2 T olive oil
- ▸ 3/4 c water
- ▸ 1/3 c soy sauce
- ▸ 1/3 c light brown sugar
- ▸ 1/4 c apple juice
- ▸ 2 T ketchup
- ▸ 1 garlic clove, minced
- ▸ 2 T cornstarch
- ▸ 1 T apple cider vinegar
- ▸ 3/4 t crushed red pepper flakes
- ▸ 1/4 t ginger

Directions

1. Heat oil in large skillet. Add chicken pieces and cook until browned.
2. In a large BlenderBottle, blend marked (▸) ingredients, add to skillet, and bring to hard boil.
3. Reduce heat and simmer for 20 minutes.

Serve over hot rice.

Nutritional Information

(per serving: 377 cal., 14.7 g total fat (3.6 g sat. fat), 135 mg chol., 989 mg sodium, 14.3 g carbo., 10.4 g sugars, 44.8 g protein)

Chile Relleno Casserole

Prep Time	Cook Time	Servings
20 minutes	15 minutes	4

Ingredients

2-3 large fresh Poblano or Anaheim chili peppers
1 1/2 c shredded Mexican-blend cheese
▸ 3 eggs
▸ 1/4 c milk
▸ 1/3 c all-purpose flour
▸ 1/2 t baking powder
▸ 1/4 t cayenne pepper
▸ 1/8 t salt
Salsa (optional)
Sour cream (optional)

Directions

1. Preheat oven to 450° F (230° C). Quarter the peppers and remove seeds, stems, and veins. Cook peppers in boiling water for 3 minutes and drain. Invert peppers on paper towels to dry. Place the peppers in a greased 8x8-inch glass baking dish. Top with 1 cup cheese.
2. In a small BlenderBottle®, combine marked (▸) ingredients and shake until smooth. Pour mixture over peppers and cheese.
3. Bake uncovered for about 15 minutes or until a knife inserted into center comes out clean. Sprinkle with remaining 1/2 cup cheese and let stand about 5 minutes or until cheese melts.

Great with fresh salsa and sour cream.

Nutritional Information
(per serving: 274 cal., 17.8 g total fat (10.2 g sat. fat), 185 mg chol., 392 mg sodium, 11.9 g carbo., 2.4 g sugars, 16.7 g protein)

Coconut Curry Tofu

Prep Time
25 minutes

Cook Time
15 minutes

Servings
6

Ingredients

- ▸ 1 (14 oz.) can light coconut milk
- ▸ 1/4 c soy sauce
- ▸ 1/2 t brown sugar
- ▸ 1 1/2 t curry powder
- ▸ 1/4 t ground ginger
- ▸ 2 t chili paste
- 1 lb. firm tofu, cut into 3/4-inch cubes
- 1 c green onions, finely chopped
- 4 Roma (plum) tomatoes, chopped
- 1 yellow bell pepper, thinly sliced
- 4 oz. fresh mushrooms, chopped
- 1/4 c fresh basil, chopped (or 4 t dried basil)
- 4 c bok choy, chopped
- Salt to taste

Directions

1. In a large BlenderBottle®, combine marked (▸) ingredients and shake well. Pour mixture into a large heavy skillet and bring to a boil.
2. Stir in tofu, tomatoes, yellow pepper, mushrooms, and green onion. Cover and cook for 5 minutes, stirring occasionally.
3. Mix in basil and bok choy. Season with salt and continue cooking for 5 minutes, or until vegetables are tender but crisp.

Tip: *Try adding chopped pineapple and peanuts to the dish for added flavor. Cooked chicken may be substituted for the tofu.*

Nutritional Information
(per serving: 256 cal., 19.7 g total fat (14.7 g sat. fat), 1 mg chol., 672 mg sodium, 14.1 g carbo., 7.5 g sugars, 11.2 g protein)

Gourmet Chicken Ranch Pizza

Prep Time	Cook Time	Makes
15 minutes	40 minutes	1 medium pizza (about 4 servings)

Ingredients

1/2 c Buttermilk Ranch Dressing (see pg. 73)
2 pre-cooked chicken breasts
1 (10 oz.) can refrigerated pizza crust
1 c shredded mozzarella cheese
1 c cheddar cheese shredded
1 c chopped tomatoes
1/4 c chopped green onions
Italian seasoning
Onion powder
Garlic powder
Salt

Directions

1. Preheat oven to 425° F (220° C). Lightly grease a pizza pan or medium baking sheet.
2. Cut or shred chicken breasts into bite-sized pieces.
3. Unroll pizza dough and press into the prepared pizza pan and bake for 7 minutes or until it begins to turn golden brown. Remove from oven.
4. Spread ranch dressing over partially baked crust. Sprinkle with mozzarella cheese, tomatoes, green onions, and chicken. Cover with cheddar cheese. Lightly dust top with Italian seasoning and garlic powder.
5. Return to oven for 20 to 30 minutes, until cheese is melted.

Nutritional Information

(per 1/4 pizza: 602 cal., 29.35 g total fat (12.6 g sat. fat), 115.5 mg chol., 1060 mg sodium, 42.5 g carbo., 7.5 g sugars, 42 g protein)

Homemade Mac N' Cheese

Prep Time	**Cook Time**	**Servings**
10 minutes	10 minutes	6

Ingredients

1 (16 oz.) package uncooked macaroni
3 T butter
▸ 2 c milk
▸ 3 T flour
▸ 1/2 t salt
▸ 1/4 t ground black pepper
2 c sharp cheddar cheese, shredded

Directions

1. Cook macaroni according to package instructions and drain.
2. While macaroni is cooking, melt butter in a medium-sized saucepan over medium heat. In a large BlenderBottle®, combine marked (▸) ingredients and blend well. Pour mixture into saucepan with butter.
3. Add cheese and stir until melted and the mixture thickens.
4. Add cheese sauce to macaroni and stir to coat. Serve immediately.

Nutritional Information
(per serving: 538 cal., 21 g total fat (12.8 g sat. fat), 61 mg chol., 507 mg sodium, 63.8 g carbo., 6.4 g sugars, 22.4 g protein)

Michael's Spinach Quiche

Prep Time	Cook Time	Servings
20 minutes	45 minutes	6

Ingredients

1 (9 inch) unbaked deep dish pie crust
1 T butter
2 cloves garlic, minced
1/2 small onion, chopped
1 c spinach, chopped (fresh or frozen)
2 c cheddar cheese, shredded
▸ 4 eggs
▸ 3/4 c milk
▸ Salt and pepper to taste

Directions

1. Preheat oven to 375° F (190° C).
2. In a medium skillet, melt butter over medium heat. Sauté onion and garlic until lightly browned. Add spinach and 1 cup of cheese. Season with salt and pepper and cook until cheese is melted. Spoon mixture into pie crust.
3. In a large BlenderBottle®, combine marked (▸) ingredients and blend well. Pour mixture into pie crust and carefully stir with spinach mixture until combined.
4. Bake for 15 minutes. Sprinkle remaining cheese on top, and bake for an additional 35 to 40 minutes until a knife inserted into middle comes out clean. Allow to stand 10 minutes before serving.

Nutritional Information

(per serving: 352 cal., 21.6 g total fat (8.6 g sat. fat), 151 mg chol., 416 mg sodium, 28.9 g carbo., 17.4 g sugars, 11.3 g protein)

Key West Chicken

Prep Time	Cook Time	Servings
15 minutes	30 minutes	8

Ingredients

8 skinless, boneless chicken breast halves

- ▸ 1/4 c soy sauce
- ▸ 2 T honey
- ▸ 2 T vegetable oil
- ▸ 1 T fresh lime juice
- ▸ 2 t minced garlic

Directions

1. Place chicken breasts in a shallow glass container. Blend marked (▸) ingredients in a small BlenderBottle® and pour over chicken breasts. Cover and marinate in refrigerator at least 30 minutes (or overnight).
2. Preheat an outdoor grill to high heat. Lightly oil the grill grate. Discard marinade and grill chicken for 6 to 8 minutes on each side, or until juices run clear.

Nutritional Information

(per serving: 375 cal., 16 g total fat (4.1 g sat. fat), 151 mg chol., 596 mg sodium, 5.3 g carbo., 4.5 g sugars, 49.8 g protein)

Mustard-Apricot Tenderloin

Prep Time	Cook Time	Servings
15 minutes	15 minutes	4

Ingredients

- ▸ 1/2 c apricot jam
- ▸ 1/4 c Dijon mustard
- 1 t garlic salt
- 1 pork tenderloin (about 1 pound)

Directions

1. Mix marked (▸) ingredients in a small BlenderBottle®. Rub tenderloin with garlic salt.
2. Grill over a medium-high heat, brushing frequently with mustard glaze, turning once or twice until just done (about 15 minutes).

Nutritional Information

(per serving: 272 cal., 4.7 g total fat (4.7 g sat. fat), 83 mg chol., 258 mg sodium, 27.1 g carbo., 17.7 g sugars, 30.8 g protein)

Potato Bacon Slow Cooker Soup

Prep Time	Cook Time	Servings
30 minutes	4.5 hours cooking (in a slow-cooker)	6

Ingredients

5 large potatoes, diced
1 onion, finely chopped
2 (10.5 oz.) cans condensed chicken broth
2 c water
1/2 t salt
1/2 t dried dill weed
1/2 t ground white pepper
1/2 c all-purpose flour
▸ 2 c half-and-half cream
▸ 1 (12 oz.) can evaporated milk
6 slices pre-cooked bacon, cut into 1/2-inch pieces

Directions

1. Add potatoes, onion, chicken broth, water, salt, dill weed, and pepper to large slow cooker. Cover and cook on high for 4 hours, stirring occasionally.
2. After soup has cooked for 4 hours, combine marked (▸) ingredients in a large BlenderBottle® and blend well. Stir BlenderBottle mixture into slow cooker. Stir in evaporated milk and bacon pieces. Cover and cook for an additional 30 minutes before serving.

Garnish with grated cheese and crumbled bacon pieces

Nutritional Information

(per serving: 608 cal., 26.4 g total fat (12.5 g sat. fat), 77 mg chol., 1279 mg sodium, 68 g carbo., 10.5 g sugars, 25 g protein)

Sloppy Joes

Prep Time	Cook Time	Servings
15 minutes	30 minutes	6

Ingredients

1 lb lean ground beef
1/2 c chopped onion
1/4 c chopped green bell pepper
▸ 3/4 c ketchup
▸ 1/4 c water
▸ 3 t brown sugar
▸ 1 t prepared yellow mustard
▸ 1/2 t garlic powder

Directions

1. In a medium skillet, brown ground beef, onion, and green pepper over medium-high heat. Drain.
2. In a small BlenderBottle®, combine marked (▸) ingredients and blend until smooth. Pour mixture into skillet and mix thoroughly with beef. Reduce heat and simmer for 20-30 minutes. Salt and pepper to taste.
3. Spoon onto warm hamburger buns and serve immediately.

Nutritional Information

(per serving: 182 cal., 4.8 g total fat (1.8 g sat. fat), 67 mg chol., 395 mg sodium, 10.3 g carbo., 8.9 g sugars, 23.7 g protein)

Zesty Apricot Chicken

Prep Time	Cook Time	Servings
10 minutes	50-60 minutes	8

Ingredients

8 boneless, skinless chicken breast halves
- ▸ 1 c apricot preserves
- ▸ 1 c French dressing
- ▸ 1 (8 oz.) package dry onion soup mix
- ▸ 1/4 c Worcestershire sauce

Directions

1. Preheat oven to 350° F (180° C).
2. Blend marked (▸) ingredients in a large BlenderBottle® until smooth.
3. Place chicken in a 9x13-inch baking dish and pour apricot mixture evenly over chicken.
4. Bake uncovered in preheated oven for 50-60 minutes or until thoroughly cooked.

Nutritional Information

(per serving: 581 cal., 17.2 g total fat (3.9 g sat. fat), 151 mg chol., 2473 mg sodium, 54.1 g carbo., 28.3 g sugars, 51.8 g protein)

Steak Salad

Prep Time
30 minutes

Servings
4

Ingredients

Dressing

- ▸ 1/3 c olive oil
- ▸ 3 T red wine vinegar
- ▸ 2 T lemon juice
- ▸ 1 clove garlic, minced
- ▸ 1/2 t salt
- ▸ 1/8 t ground black pepper
- ▸ 1 t Worcestershire sauce

Salad

1 3/4 lbs. beef sirloin steak, grilled
3/4 c crumbled blue cheese
8 c romaine lettuce, chopped
2 tomatoes, sliced
1 small green bell pepper, sliced
1 carrot, sliced
1/2 c red onion, sliced
1/4 c pimento-stuffed green olives, sliced

Directions

1. In a small BlenderBottle®, combine marked (▸) ingredients and blend well. Place in refrigerator.
2. In a large salad bowl, combine lettuce, tomato, green pepper, onion, olives, and blue cheese.
3. Cut steak into bite-sized strips and add to salad. Add dressing and toss to coat.

Nutritional Information
(per serving: 678 cal., 38.8 g total fat (12.2 g sat. fat), 196 mg chol., 891 mg sodium, 12 g carbo., 6.5 g sugars, 67.9 g protein)

Bacon Ranch Pasta Salad

Prep Time	Chill Time	Servings
25 minutes	1 hour	8

Ingredients

1 (12 oz.) package uncooked tri-color rotini pasta
10 slices cooked bacon, chopped
▸ 1 c mayonnaise
▸ 3 T dry ranch salad dressing mix
▸ 1/4 t garlic powder
▸ 1/4 t ground black pepper
▸ 1/2 c milk
1 large tomato, chopped
1 (4.25 oz.) can sliced black olives
1 c cheddar cheese, shredded

Directions

1. Bring a large pot of lightly salted water to a boil. Stir in rotini pasta and cook until al dente. Drain.
2. Combine cooked pasta, tomato, bacon, black olives, and cheese in a large bowl.
3. In a large BlenderBottle®, combine marked (▸) ingredients and mix until smooth. Pour dressing over salad and toss to coat. Cover and refrigerate for at least 1 hour before serving.

Nutritional Information
(per serving: 517 cal., 32.3 g total fat (9.8 g sat. fat), 94 mg chol., 1297 mg sodium, 34 g carbo., 3.5 g sugars, 22.7 g protein)

Greek Salad

Prep Time
15 minutes

Servings
6 side dish servings

Ingredients

Dressing

- ▸ 2 T olive oil
- ▸ 2 T lemon juice
- ▸ 2 t snipped fresh oregano (or 1/2 t dried oregano)
- ▸ 1/8 t salt
- ▸ 1/8 t ground black pepper

Salad

6 c romaine lettuce or mixed salad greens
8 cherry tomatoes, halved (or 2 medium tomatoes, cut into wedges)
1 small cucumber, halved lengthwise and thinly sliced
1 small red onion, cut into thin wedges
1/2 c pitted kalamata olives
1/2 c crumbled feta cheese

Directions

1. In a large salad bowl, combine salad greens, tomato, onion, cucumber, olives, and feta cheese.
2. In a small BlenderBottle®, combine marked (▸) ingredients and blend well. Pour over salad and toss to coat.

Serve immediately.

Nutritional Information
(per serving: 138 cal., 8.9 g total fat (2.7 g sat. fat), 11 mg chol., 303 mg sodium, 13 g carbo., 7.4 g sugars, 4.3 g protein)

Mandarin Almond Chicken Salad

Prep Time
45 minutes

Servings
6

Ingredients

Dressing

- ▸ 1/2 c vegetable oil
- ▸ 1/2 c corn syrup
- ▸ 3 T white distilled vinegar
- ▸ 2 T pineapple juice
- ▸ 4 t granulated sugar
- ▸ 1 T light brown sugar
- ▸ 1 T rice wine vinegar
- ▸ 1 T soy sauce
- ▸ 1 t sesame oil
- ▸ 1/2 t sesame seeds
- ▸ 1/4 t ground mustard
- ▸ 1/4 t ground ginger
- ▸ 1/8 t salt
- ▸ 1/8 t paprika
- ▸ 1 dash garlic powder
- ▸ 1 dash ground black pepper

Salad

4 pre-cooked chicken breasts, diced
1 head iceberg lettuce, chopped
4 cups red leaf lettuce, chopped
1 1/3 cups canned mandarin orange segments
1 c dry chow mein noodles
1 c sliced almonds

Directions

1. In a small BlenderBottle®, combine marked (▸) ingredients and blend.
2. Place remaining ingredients in a large bowl, drizzle with dressing, and toss to coat. Serve immediately.

Nutritional Information
(per serving: 620 cal., 33 g total fat (6 g sat. fat), 97 mg chol., 332 mg sodium, 40 g carbo., 19 g sugars, 41 g protein)

Mandarin Cream Fruit Salad

Prep Time	Chill Time	Servings
10 minutes	2 hours	8

Ingredients

- ▸ 1 1/2 c milk
- ▸ 1/3 c orange juice concentrate, thawed
- ▸ 1 (3.5 oz.) package instant vanilla pudding mix
- ▸ 3/4c sour cream
- 1 red apple, peeled, cored, and sliced
- 2 bananas, sliced
- 1 (20 oz.) can pineapple tidbits, drained
- 1 (15 oz.) can sliced peaches, drained
- 1 (11 oz.) can mandarin orange segments, drained

Directions

1. In a large BlenderBottle®, combine marked (▸) ingredients and blend until smooth.
2. Combine fruits in a large salad bowl.
3. Pour BlenderBottle mixture over fruit and gently toss until coated. Chill for at least two hours before serving.

Nutritional Information

(per serving: 226 cal., 5.9 g total fat (3.5 g sat. fat), 13 mg chol., 212 mg sodium, 42.9 g carbo., 34.2 g sugars, 3.7 g protein)

Quick Confetti Pasta Salad

Prep Time	Chill Time	Servings
10 minutes	1-2 hours	6

Ingredients

2 c colored rotini pasta, cooked
▸ 1 c real mayonnaise
▸ 1 T red wine vinegar
▸ 1 1/2 T finely chopped fresh basil
▸ 1 t salt
▸ 1/4 t ground black pepper
▸ 1 clove garlic, minced
1 c tomatoes, chopped
1/2 c yellow bell peppers, chopped
1/2 c sliced black olives
6 oz. feta cheese, crumbled (optional)

Directions

1. In a small BlenderBottle®, combine marked (▸) ingredients and mix until well blended.
2. Place remaining ingredients in a large mixing bowl and toss with BlenderBottle mixture.
3. Chill several hours. Mix gently before serving. For best flavor, chill overnight.

Nutritional Information

(per serving: 353 cal., 20.8 g total fat (6.4 g sat. fat), 35 mg chol., 1084 mg sodium, 33.8 g carbo., 5.4 g sugars, 8.5 g protein)

Santa Fe Rice Salad

Prep Time
30 minutes

Servings
8

Ingredients

2 c cooked white rice
2 c black beans, drained and rinsed
2 large tomatoes, seeded and diced
2 c cheddar cheese, cubed
2/3 c sliced green onions
▸ 2/3 c vegetable oil
▸ 1/2 c vinegar
▸ 2 T jalapeno peppers, minced
▸ 1 t white sugar
▸ Salt to taste
2 avocados, peeled, pitted, and diced

Directions

1. In a large bowl, mix together rice, beans, tomato, cheese, and green onion.
2. In a small BlenderBottle®, mix marked (▸) ingredients and pour over rice mixture. Toss to coat.
3. Cover and refrigerate for 30 minutes. Top with avocado just before serving.

Nutritional Information
(per serving: 706 cal., 36 g total fat (11 g sat. fat), 30 mg chol., 235 mg sodium, 75 g carbo., 3.6 g sugars, 22.4 g protein)

Bacon & Broccoli Salad

Prep Time	Chill Time	Servings
15 minutes	2 hours	6

Ingredients

10 slices bacon, precooked, crumbled
1 head fresh broccoli, cut into bite-size pieces
1/4 c red onion, chopped
1/2 c raisins
1 c sunflower seeds
▸ 3 T white wine vinegar
▸ 2 T white sugar
▸ 1 c mayonnaise

Directions

1. In a medium bowl, combine the broccoli, onion, raisins, bacon, and sunflower seeds.
2. Blend marked (▸) ingredients in a small BlenderBottle® until smooth. Pour over broccoli mixture and toss until well mixed.
3. Cover and refrigerate salad for at least 2 hours.

Nutritional Information

(per serving: 524 cal., 37 g total fat (8.8 g sat. fat), 62 mg chol., 1387 mg sodium, 28.8 g carbo., 15 g sugars, 21 g protein)

Strawberry Spinach Salad

Prep Time	Chill Time	Servings
15 minutes	1 hour	4

Ingredients

- ▸ 2 T sesame seeds
- ▸ 1 T poppy seeds
- ▸ 1/2 c white sugar
- ▸ 1/2 c olive oil
- ▸ 1/4 c distilled white vinegar
- ▸ 1/4 t paprika
- ▸ 1/4 t Worcestershire sauce
- ▸ 1/8 t onion powder
- 10 oz. fresh spinach - rinsed, dried and torn into bite-size pieces
- 1 quart strawberries - cleaned, hulled and sliced
- 1/4 c almonds, slivered

Directions

1. Mix marked (▸) ingredients in a small BlenderBottle®. Chill dressing for 1 hour.
2. In a large salad bowl, combine spinach, strawberries, and almonds. Pour dressing over salad and toss to coat. Refrigerate 10 to 15 minutes before serving.

Nutritional Information

(per serving: 474 cal., 33.9 g total fat (4.4 g sat. fat), 0 mg chol., 64 mg sodium, 41.8 g carbo., 33 g sugars, 5.5 g protein)

Sweet Creamy Coleslaw

Prep Time	Chill Time	Servings
15 minutes	1 hour	8

Ingredients

1 (16 oz.) bag coleslaw mix
2 T diced onion
▸ 2/3 c mayonnaise
▸ 3 T vegetable oil
▸ 3 T milk
▸ 1/2 c white sugar
▸ 1 T white wine vinegar
▸ 1/4 t salt
▸ 1/2 t poppy seeds

Directions

1. Add coleslaw mix and onion in a large bowl.
2. Blend marked (▸) ingredients in a small BlenderBottle®. Pour dressing over coleslaw mix and toss to coat. Cover and refrigerate for at least 1 hour before serving.

Nutritional Information

(per serving: 219 cal., 13.3 g total fat (2.3 g sat. fat), 10 mg chol., 228 mg sodium, 24.8 g carbo., 14 g sugars, 1.2 g protein)

Buttermilk Ranch Dressing

Prep Time
5 minutes

Makes Approximately
1 1/2 cups

Ingredients

- ▸ 1/2 c buttermilk
- ▸ 1 c mayonnaise
- ▸ 1/4 t fresh ground black pepper
- ▸ 1/8 t paprika
- ▸ 1/8 t garlic powder
- ▸ 1 T powdered ranch dressing mix

Directions

1. Combine marked (▸) ingredients in a large BlenderBottle® and blend until smooth. To maximize flavor, chill at least one hour before serving.

Tip: *Great with cheese fries!*

Nutritional Information

(per 2T serving: 81 cal., 6.6 g total fat (1 g sat. fat), 6 mg chol., 157 mg sodium, 5.3 g carbo., 1.8 g sugars, 0.6 g protein)

Caesar Salad Dressing

Prep Time
5 minutes

Makes Approximately
1 1/2 cups

Ingredients

- 1 c mayonnaise
- 1/2 c Parmesan cheese
- 1 T lemon juice
- 1 t Worcestershire sauce
- 1 clove garlic, minced
- 4 T milk
- 1/4 t salt
- 1/8 t ground black pepper

Directions

1. Combine marked (▸) ingredients in a large BlenderBottle® and blend until smooth.

Nutritional Information
(per 2 T serving: 98 cal., 7.8 g total fat (1.7 g sat. fat), 9 mg chol., 261 mg sodium, 5.4 g carbo., 1.7 g sugars, 2 g protein)

Fresh French Salad Dressing

Prep Time
10 minutes

Makes Approximately
3 cups

Ingredients

- 1 c vegetable oil
- 1/2 c ketchup
- 1/2 c sugar
- 1/2 c red wine vinegar
- 1 t onion powder
- 1 t paprika
- 1/2 t Worcestershire sauce
- Salt and pepper to taste

Directions

1. Combine marked (▸) ingredients in a large BlenderBottle® and blend until smooth.

Nutritional Information
(per 2 T serving: 24 cal., 9 g total fat (2 g sat. fat), 0 mg chol., 59 mg sodium, 6 g carbo., 6 g sugars, 0.2 g protein)

Creamy Italian Dressing

Prep Time
10 minutes

Makes Approximately
1 cup

Ingredients

- ▸ 1 c mayonnaise
- ▸ 2 T red wine vinegar
- ▸ 1 T sugar
- ▸ 1 1/2 t onion powder
- ▸ 3/4 t Italian seasoning
- ▸ 1/4 t garlic powder
- ▸ 1/4 t salt
- ▸ 1/8 t ground black pepper

Directions

1. Combine marked (▸) ingredients in a large BlenderBottle® and blend until smooth.

Nutritional Information

(per 2 T serving: 125 cal., 10 g total fat (1.5 g sat. fat), 8 mg chol., 283 mg sodium, 9.1 g carbo., 3.7 g sugars, 0.3 g protein)

Snappy Thousand Island Dressing

Prep Time
5 minutes

Makes Approximately
3 cups

Ingredients

- ▸ 1 c mayonnaise
- ▸ 1/4 c water
- ▸ 1/2 c ketchup
- ▸ 1 c sweet pickle relish
- ▸ 1 pinch salt
- ▸ 1 pinch ground black pepper

Directions

1. Combine marked (▸) ingredients in a large BlenderBottle® and blend until smooth.

Nutritional Information

(per 2 T serving: 56 cal., 3.3 g total fat (0 g sat. fat), 3 mg chol., 216 mg sodium, 7.2 g carbo., 4.7 g sugars, 0.2 g protein)

Fresh Garlic Balsamic Vinaigrette

Prep Time
5 minutes

Makes Approximately
1 cup

Ingredients

- ▸ 3/4 c olive oil
- ▸ 1/4 c balsamic vinegar
- ▸ 3 T honey
- ▸ 2 cloves of garlic, minced
- ▸ 1/2 t lemon juice
- ▸ 1/2 t salt

Directions

1. Combine marked (▸) ingredients in a large BlenderBottle® and blend until smooth.

Nutritional Information

(per serving: 206 cal., 20 g total fat (2.8 g sat. fat), 149 mg chol., 149 mg sodium, 6.8 g carbo., 6.5 g sugars, 0.1 g protein)

Honey Mustard Dressing

Prep Time
5 minutes

Makes Approximately
1 cup

Ingredients

- ▸ 1/2 c mayonnaise
- ▸ 2 T prepared mustard
- ▸ 2 T honey
- ▸ 1 T lemon juice

Directions

1. Combine marked (▸) ingredients in a large BlenderBottle® and blend until smooth.

Nutritional Information

(per 2 T serving: 76 cal., 5.1 g total fat (0.7 g sat. fat), 4 mg chol., 147 mg sodium, 8.2 g carbo., 5.3 g sugars, 0.3 g protein)

Poppy Seed Dressing

Prep Time
5 minutes

Makes Approximately
2 1/2 cups

Ingredients

- ▸ 1 c vegetable oil
- ▸ 3/4 c sugar
- ▸ 1/3 c cider vinegar
- ▸ 4 1/2 t onion, grated (or 1/4 t onion powder)
- ▸ 3 t ground mustard
- ▸ 1 t poppy seeds
- ▸ 1/2 t salt

Directions

1. Combine marked (▸) ingredients in a large BlenderBottle® and blend until smooth.

Nutritional Information
(per 2T serving: 130 cal., 11 g total fat (2.2 g sat. fat), 0 mg chol., 62 mg sodium, 8 g carbo., 7.6 g sugars, 0.2 g protein)

Zippy Ginger Salad Dressing

Prep Time
5 minutes

Makes Approximately
1 cup

Ingredients

- ▸ 1/4 c rice vinegar
- ▸ 1/4 c vegetable oil
- ▸ 1/4 c sesame oil
- ▸ 3 T hot chili oil
- ▸ 4 tsp soy sauce
- ▸ 3 T fresh ground ginger
- ▸ 1/4 t garlic powder
- ▸ 1/4 t salt (or to taste)

Directions

1. Combine marked (▸) ingredients in a large BlenderBottle® and blend until smooth.

Nutritional Information
(per 2T serving: 179 cal., 19 g total fat (3.1 g sat. fat), 0 mg chol., 224 mg sodium, 1.7 g carbo., 0 g sugars, 0.4 g protein)

Best Steak Marinade

Prep Time
10 minutes

Servings
6

Ingredients

- ▸ 1/3 c soy sauce
- ▸ 1/2 c olive oil
- ▸ 1/3 c lemon juice
- ▸ 1/4 c Worcestershire sauce
- ▸ 1 1/2 T garlic powder
- ▸ 3 T dried basil
- ▸ 1 1/2 T dried parsley flakes
- ▸ 1 t ground white pepper

Directions

1. Combine marked (▸) ingredients in a large BlenderBottle® and blend until smooth.

Marinate steaks in a glass bowl or dish in the refrigerator for 8 hours before cooking.

Nutritional Information
(per serving (marinade only): 63 cal., 6 g total fat (0.8 g sat. fat), 0 mg chol., 310 mg sodium, 2 g carbo., 1 g sugars, 0.5 g protein)

Tasty Teriyaki Sauce

Prep Time
10 minutes

Makes Approximately
1 1/2 cups

Ingredients

- ▸ 3/4 c water
- ▸ 1/4 c and 2 T soy sauce
- ▸ 3/4 c brown sugar
- ▸ 1/4 t garlic powder
- ▸ 1/8 t ground ginger
- ▸ 2 T corn starch

Tip: *Pour over a bowl of sliced chicken, steamed vegetables, and hot rice for a delicious Teriyaki chicken bowl, or use as a dipping sauce for fried chicken strips!*

Directions

1. Combine marked (▸) ingredients in a small BlenderBottle® and blend until smooth.
2. Pour mixture into a small saucepan and carefully bring to a boil over medium-high heat, stirring regularly. Reduce heat and simmer for 5 minutes or until sauce reaches desired consistency.

Nutritional Information
(per 1/4 cup serving: 90 cal., 0 g total fat (0 g sat. fat), 0 mg chol., 906 mg sodium, 22.1 g carbo., 17.9 g sugars, 1 g protein)

Dad's Five-Star Chicken Marinade

Prep Time
10 minutes

Servings
6

Ingredients

- ▸ 1 1/2 c vegetable oil
- ▸ 3/4 c soy sauce
- ▸ 1/2 c Worcestershire sauce
- ▸ 1/2 c red wine vinegar
- ▸ 1/3 c lemon juice
- ▸ 2 T dry mustard
- ▸ 1 t salt
- ▸ 1 T black pepper
- ▸ 1 1/2 t finely minced fresh parsley

Directions

1. Combine marked (▸) ingredients in a large BlenderBottle® and blend until smooth.

Tip: *Always use a glass dish for marinating. For best flavor, allow chicken to marinate in the refrigerator for 1-3 hours before grilling.*

Nutritional Information

(per serving (marinade only): 182 cal., 18.5 g total fat (3.6 g sat. fat), 0 mg chol., 814 mg sodium, 3.3 g carbo., 1.7 g sugars, 1 g protein)

Never Fail BlenderBottle® Gravy

Prep Time
15 minutes

Makes Approximately
2 cups

Ingredients

- ▸ 1 1/2 c water
- ▸ 3 t beef bouillon powder
- ▸ 1/4 c all-purpose flour
- ▸ 1 T onion powder
- ▸ 1/4 c melted butter
- ▸ 1/2 t ground black pepper

Tip: *For chicken gravy, substitute chicken bouillon for beef bouillon.*

Directions

1. Combine marked (▸) ingredients in a large BlenderBottle and shake until smooth
2. Pour mixture into a small saucepan. Bring gravy to a boil over medium-high heat, stirring constantly with a wire whisk.

Nutritional Information

(per 1/4 cup serving: 69 cal., 5.8 g total fat (3.6 g sat. fat), 15 mg chol., 53 mg sodium, 3.8 g carbo., 0 g sugars, 0.6 g protein)

Cheese Sauce

Prep Time
15 minutes

Makes Approximately
1 1/2 cups

Ingredients

2 T butter or margarine
▸ 1 1/2 c milk
▸ 2 T all-purpose flour
▸ Dash ground black pepper
1 1/2 c shredded American, processed Swiss, or Gruyère cheese

Tip: *For further variations, try 1/2 c crumbled blue cheese or 3/4 c grated Parmesan cheese instead of American.*

Directions

1. Melt butter in a medium saucepan over medium heat.
2. Combine marked (▸) ingredients in a small BlenderBottle® and blend until smooth. Add mixture to saucepan.
3. Over medium heat, stir in cheese until melted. Drizzle over steamed vegetables and serve immediately.

Nutritional Information
(per 1/4 cup serving (American cheese): 167 cal., 12.2 g total fat (7.4 g sat. fat), 38 mg chol., 410 mg sodium, 7 g carbo., 5.2 g sugars, 7.5 g protein)

Sweet N' Tangy Buffalo Wing Dip

Prep Time
10 minutes

Makes Approximately
1 1/4 cups

Ingredients

▸ 1/2 c melted butter
▸ 1/3 c hot pepper sauce
▸ 1/3 c ketchup
▸ 2 T honey

Tip: *Makes a great dip for Crispy Buffalo Wings (pg. 19) or fried chicken strips.*

Directions

1. Combine marked (▸) ingredients in a small BlenderBottle® and blend until smooth.
2. Pour mixture into a small saucepan and bring to a boil over medium-high heat, stirring regularly. Reduce heat and simmer for about 10 minutes or until sauce reaches desired thickness.

Nutritional Information
(per 1/4 cup serving: 206 cal., 18.6 g total fat (11.7 g sat. fat), 49 mg chol., 407 mg sodium, 11.1 g carbo., 10.6 g sugars, 0.7 g protein)

Cocktail Sauce

Prep Time
5 minutes

Makes Approximately
1 cup

Ingredients

- ▸ 3/4 c bottled chili sauce
- ▸ 2 T lemon juice
- ▸ 2 T green onion, thinly sliced
- ▸ 1 T prepared horseradish
- ▸ 2 t Worcestershire sauce
- ▸ Several dashes hot pepper sauce

Directions

1. Combine marked (▸) ingredients in a small BlenderBottle® and blend until smooth. Store in BlenderBottle in refrigerator for up to two weeks.

Nutritional Information
(per 1/8 cup serving: 6 cal., 0.1 g total fat (0 g sat. fat), 0 mg chol., 597 mg sodium, 1.3 g carbo., 0.8 g sugars, 0.2 g protein)

Herb-Garlic Sauce

Prep Time
15 minutes

Makes Approximately
1 1/2 cups

Ingredients

- 2 T butter or margarine
- ▸ 1 1/2 c milk
- ▸ 2 T all-purpose flour
- ▸ 1/4 t garlic powder
- ▸ 1/2 t basil, dried, crushed
- ▸ 1/2 t oregano, dried, crushed
- ▸ 1/4 t salt
- ▸ Dash ground black pepper

Directions

1. Melt butter in a medium saucepan over medium heat.
2. Combine marked (▸) ingredients in a small BlenderBottle® and blend until smooth. Add mixture to saucepan, stirring constantly.
3. Continue to cook over medium heat, stirring frequently, until sauce thickens to desired consistency. Serve with vegetables or poultry.

Nutritional Information
(per 1/4 cup serving: 75 cal., 5.1 g total fat (3.2 g sat. fat), 15 mg chol., 149 mg sodium, 5 g carbo., 3.1 g sugars, 2.3 g protein)

Fast & Easy Pizza Sauce

Prep Time
5 minutes

Makes Approximately
2 1/2 cups

Ingredients

- ▸ 1 (15 oz.) can tomato sauce
- ▸ 1 (6 oz.) can tomato paste
- ▸ 1 t dried oregano
- ▸ 1 t garlic salt
- ▸ 1 t basil
- ▸ 1/2 t sugar

Directions

1. Combine marked (▸) ingredients in a large BlenderBottle® and blend until smooth.

Makes enough sauce for approximately 2 pizzas.

Nutritional Information
(per 1/4 cup serving: 26 cal., 0.2 g total fat (0 g sat. fat), 0 mg chol., 240 mg sodium, 6 g carbo., 4.2 g sugars, 1.4 g protein)

Honey Mustard Sauce

Prep Time
5 minutes

Makes Approximately
1 cup

Ingredients

- ▸ 1/2 c Dijon mustard
- ▸ 1/2 c honey
- ▸ 2 T mayonnaise
- ▸ 1 T lemon juice
- ▸ Salt and pepper to taste

Directions

1. Combine marked (▸) ingredients in a small BlenderBottle® and blend until smooth.

Tip: *This kid-favorite sauce makes a great dip for fried chicken strips or chicken nuggets.*

Nutritional Information
(per 1/4 cup serving: 179 cal., 3.7 g total fat (0 g sat. fat), 2 mg chol., 409 mg sodium, 38.7 g carbo., 35.6 g sugars, 1.6 g protein)

Savory Barbecue Sauce

Prep Time
15 minutes

Makes Approximately
2 cups

Ingredients

- ▸ 1/2 c ketchup
- ▸ 1/2 c tomato sauce
- ▸ 1/4 c brown sugar
- ▸ 1/4 c red wine vinegar
- ▸ 1/8 c molasses
- ▸ 1 t butter, melted
- ▸ 1 t hickory-flavored liquid smoke
- ▸ 1/8 t garlic powder
- ▸ 1/8 t onion powder
- ▸ 1/4 t paprika
- ▸ 1/8 t celery seed
- ▸ 1/8 t cayenne pepper
- ▸ 1/4 t salt
- ▸ 1/4 t ground black pepper
- ▸ Dash chili powder
- ▸ Dash cinnamon

Directions

1. Combine marked (▸) ingredients in a large BlenderBottle® and blend until smooth.

Tip: *Brush sauce on your favorite meat during the last 10 minutes of cooking, or as sauce on a pizza with shredded chicken for a great barbecue chicken pizza.*

Nutritional Information
(per 1/2 cup serving: 119 cal., 1.7 g total fat (0.9 g sat. fat), 4 mg chol., 660 mg sodium, 26.3 g carbo., 22.8 g sugars, 1 g protein)

Stir Fry Sauce

Prep Time
15 minutes

Makes Approximately
1 1/2 cups

Ingredients

- ▸ 2/3 c soy sauce, low sodium
- ▸ 1/2 c chicken or vegetable broth
- ▸ 1/3 c rice vinegar
- ▸ 2 T cornstarch
- ▸ 1/4 c water
- ▸ 3 T sugar
- ▸ 1 T sesame oil
- ▸ 1/4 t white pepper
- ▸ 1 T minced garlic
- ▸ 1 T minced ginger

Directions

1. Mix marked (▸) ingredients in a large BlenderBottle® and pour mixture into a medium saucepan.
2. Bring mixture to a boil, reduce heat to medium, and cook until sauce reaches desired consistency.

Nutritional Information
(per 1/2 cup serving: 203 cal., 5.4 g total fat (0.9 g sat. fat), 18 mg chol., 3211 mg sodium, 24.1 g carbo., 13.6 g sugars, 10.7 g protein)

Sweet 'n Sour Sauce

Prep Time
10 minutes

Makes Approximately
1 1/2 cups

Ingredients

- ▸ 1/2 c packed brown sugar
- ▸ 4 t cornstarch
- ▸ 1/2 c chicken broth
- ▸ 1/3 c red wine vinegar
- ▸ 2 T corn syrup
- ▸ 2 T soy sauce
- ▸ 1 1/2 t grated fresh ginger (or 1/4 t ground ginger)
- ▸ 1 clove garlic, minced

Directions

1. Combine marked (▸) ingredients in a small BlenderBottle® and blend until smooth.
2. Pour into a small saucepan and cook over medium heat, stirring occasionally, until thickened and bubbly.

Serve warm with egg or spring rolls, or use in recipes calling for sweet-and-sour sauce.

Nutritional Information
(per 1/4 cup serving: 82 cal., 0 g total fat (0 g sat. fat), 0 mg chol., 369 mg sodium, 19.4 g carbo., 13.6 g sugars, 1 g protein)

Bread Pudding

Prep Time	Cook Time	Servings
30 minutes	45 minutes cooking	12

Ingredients

- 6 slices of bread
- ▸ 2 T butter, melted
- ▸ 4 eggs
- ▸ 2 c milk
- ▸ 3/4 c white sugar
- ▸ 1 t ground cinnamon
- ▸ 1 t vanilla extract
- 1/2 c raisins (optional)

Directions

1. Preheat oven to 350° F (175° C). Lightly grease an 8x8-inch baking dish.
2. Break bread into small pieces and place in lightly greased baking dish. Sprinkle with raisins (optional).
3. In a large BlenderBottle®, combine marked (▸) ingredients and shake until smooth. Pour over bread and lightly push down with a fork until bread is covered and soaking up the egg mixture.
4. Bake in preheated oven for 45 minutes, or until the top springs back when lightly tapped.

Nutritional Information

(per serving: 138 cal., 4.4 g total fat (2.2 g sat. fat), 70 mg chol., 82 mg sodium, 22 g carbo., 18.5 g sugars, 4 g protein)

Crème Brûlée

Prep Time	Cook Time	Chill Time	Servings
30 minutes	30 minutes	3 hours	6

Ingredients

- 3 c heavy cream
- 2 vanilla beans (or 2 T vanilla extract)
- ▸ 8 egg yolks
- ▸ 1/2 c white sugar
- 1 T white sugar (for topping)

Directions

1. In a medium saucepan, gradually heat cream with vanilla over medium heat until bubbles begin to form at edges. Remove from heat and let sit for 30 minutes.
2. In a large BlenderBottle®, blend marked (▸) ingredients. Remove vanilla beans from cream (if used) and add egg yolk mixture.
3. Cook over low heat (without boiling) until mixture thickens and coats the back of a metal spoon. Remove and evenly divide mixture among 6 ramekins or custard cups. Cover and refrigerate for 3 hours, until set.
4. Prior to serving, sprinkle remaining sugar evenly over custards and brown with a kitchen torch. Start from the outside and work inwards, constantly moving torch so as to not burn the sugar.

Tip: *If you don't have a kitchen torch, brown the sugar top under the oven broiler for a few minutes.*

Nutritional Information

(per serving: 364 cal., 28 g total fat (16 g sat. fat), 362 mg chol., 34 mg sodium, 22 g carbo., 20 g sugars, 5 g protein)

Delicious Lemon Bars

Prep Time	Cook Time	Servings
20 minutes	40 minutes	18

Ingredients

- 1/2 c butter, melted
- 1/4 c white sugar
- 1 c all-purpose flour
- ▸ 2 eggs
- ▸ 3/4 c white sugar
- ▸ 3 T all-purpose flour
- ▸ 1/3 c lemon juice
- 2 T powdered sugar

Directions

1. Preheat oven to 350° F (175° C). Grease an 8x8-inch baking dish.
2. In a medium bowl, stir together 1 cup of flour with 1/4 cup white sugar. Mix in melted butter. Press mixture into the bottom of prepared dish and bake for 15 minutes, or until golden brown.
3. In a large BlenderBottle®, combine marked (▸) ingredients and blend until smooth. Pour over prepared crust and return dish to oven.
4. Bake for an additional 20 minutes or until bars are set. Allow to cool completely before cutting into squares. Dust with powdered sugar and serve.

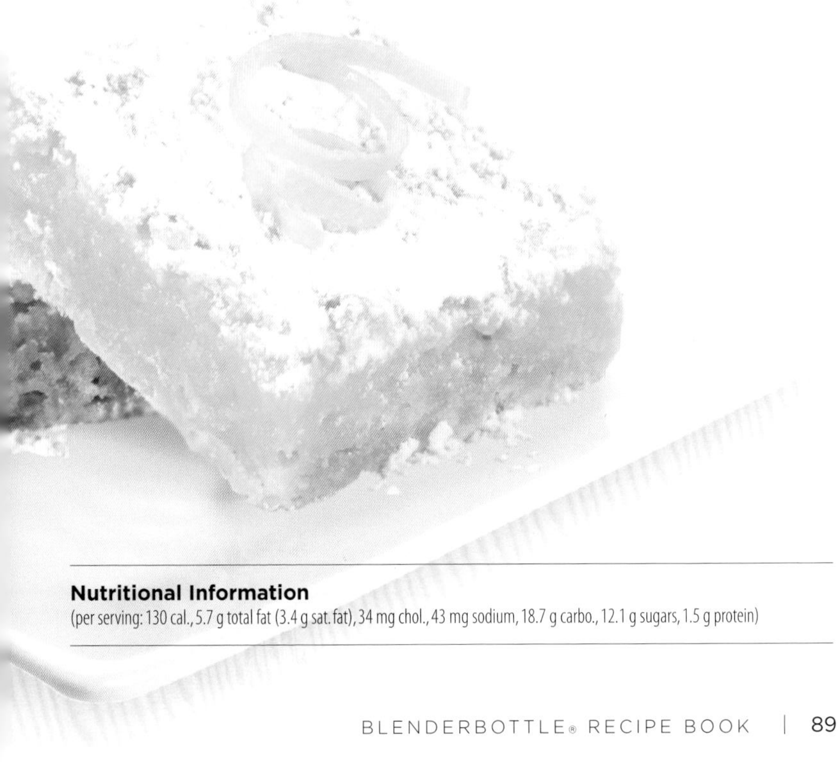

Nutritional Information

(per serving: 130 cal., 5.7 g total fat (3.4 g sat. fat), 34 mg chol., 43 mg sodium, 18.7 g carbo., 12.1 g sugars, 1.5 g protein)

Easy Peach Cobbler

Prep Time	Cook Time	Servings
15 minutes	40 minutes	6

Ingredients

2 c peaches, peeled and sliced
▸ 1 c self-rising flour*
▸ 1 c sugar
▸ 1 c milk
1/2 c butter

Cherry Cobbler

For a great cherry cobbler, follow recipe for peach cobbler but replace peaches with 1/4 cup sugar and 2 (14.5 oz.) cans red tart cherries, drained.

Mixed Berry Cobbler

Follow recipe for peach cobbler and substitute 3 cups mixed berries for peaches to make a delicious mixed berry cobbler.

Directions

1. Preheat oven to 350° F (180° C). Place butter in an 8x8-inch glass baking dish and allow to melt while oven preheats.
2. Remove dish when butter melts and add peaches.
3. In a large BlenderBottle®, mix marked (▸) ingredients until smooth. Pour over top of peaches. Do not stir.
4. Bake for 40 to 45 minutes or until top is golden brown.

Tip: *Serve warm with vanilla ice cream.*

***Note:** *If you don't have any self-rising flour, mix 1 cup all-purpose flour with 1 1/2 teaspoons baking powder and 1/2 teaspoon salt.*

Nutritional Information

(Peach: per serving: 383 cal., 16.5 g total fat (10 g sat. fat), 44 mg chol., 126 mg sodium, 56.5 g carbo., 40 g sugars, 4 g protein)
(Cherry: per serving: 551 cal., 16.5 g total fat (10 g sat. fat), 44 mg chol., 151 mg sodium, 98 g carbo., 43 g sugars, 4 g protein)
(Mixed Berry: per serving: 396 cal., 16.5 g total fat (10 g sat. fat), 44 mg chol., 126 mg sodium, 59 g carbo., 40 g sugars, 4 g protein)

Cake Batter Ice Cream

Prep Time	Freeze Time	Servings
5 minutes	30 minutes (in ice cream maker)	8

Ingredients

- ▸ 3/4 c whole milk
- ▸ 1/2 c granulated sugar
- ▸ 1 3/4 c heavy cream
- ▸ 1 t pure vanilla extract
- ▸ 1/2 c cake mix (confetti, white, or yellow)

Directions

1. In a large BlenderBottle®, combine marked (▸) ingredients in order and mix until well blended.
2. Pour into ice cream maker and freeze according to manufacturer's instructions.

Nutritional Information

(per serving: 193 cal., 10.5 g total fat (6.5 g sat. fat), 38 mg chol., 19 mg sodium, 23 g carbo., 20 g sugars, 1.7 g protein)

Classic Vanilla Ice Cream

Prep Time	Freeze Time	Servings
5 minutes	30-40 minutes (in ice cream maker)	4

Ingredients

- ▸ 2 c half-and-half
- ▸ 1 c heavy cream
- ▸ 1 T vanilla extract
- ▸ 2/3 c sugar
- ▸ 1 dash salt

Directions

1. Combine marked (▸) ingredients in a large BlenderBottle® and blend until smooth.
2. Pour mixture into ice cream maker and freeze according to manufacturer's instructions.

Nutritional Information

(per serving: 399 cal., 25 g total fat (15 g sat. fat), 86 mg chol., 100 mg sodium, 40 g carbo., 34 g sugars, 4 g protein)

Pina Colada Sorbet

Prep Time	Freeze Time	Servings
5 minutes	30-40 minutes (in ice cream maker)	8

Ingredients

- ▸ 1 3/4 c pineapple juice
- ▸ 1 1/2 c cream of coconut

For a refreshing Coconut Lime variation, use the following ingredients:

1 (16 oz.) can of cream of coconut
1/2 c fresh lime juice
3/4 c cold water
1 T lime zest

Directions

1. Combine marked (▸) ingredients in a large BlenderBottle® and blend until smooth.
2. Pour mixture into ice cream maker and freeze according to manufacturer's instructions.

Important: *When finished, allow sorbet to sit in freezer for a few hours to harden and allow flavors to blend.*

Nutritional Information

(**Piña Colada:** per serving: 177 cal., 16 g total fat (13 g sat. fat), 0 mg chol., 3 mg sodium, 10 g carbo., 5.5 g sugars, 1.8 g protein)
(**Coconut Lime:** per serving: 191 cal., 20 g total fat (17 g sat. fat), 0 mg chol., 3 mg sodium, 5 g carbo., 0 g sugars, 2.1 g protein)

Shredded Chocolate Mint Ice Cream

Prep Time	Freeze Time	Servings
5 minutes	30-40 minutes (in ice cream maker)	4

Ingredients

- ▸ 1 c 2% milk
- ▸ 1 c heavy cream
- ▸ 1/2 c sugar
- ▸ 1/4 t salt
- ▸ 1/2 t vanilla extract
- ▸ 1/2 t peppermint extract
- ▸ 1-1/2 drops green food coloring (optional)
- 1 regular size milk chocolate bar

Directions

1. Combine marked (▸) ingredients in a large BlenderBottle® and blend until smooth.
2. Pour mixture into ice cream maker and freeze according to manufacturer's instructions.
3. Using a cheese grater, shred chocolate bar into small pieces. Approximately 10 minutes into freezing process, add shredded chocolate to ice cream mixture.

Nutritional Information

(per serving: 290 cal., 15 g total fat (10 g sat. fat), 48 mg chol., 192 mg sodium, 35 g carbo., 34 g sugars, 4 g protein)

Candy Bar Pie

Prep Time	Chill Time	Servings
10 minutes	1 Hour	8

Ingredients

- 1 (10-inch) graham cracker or chocolate pie crust
- ▸ 1 (3.9 oz.) package instant chocolate pudding
- ▸ 2 c cold milk
- 1-2 candy bars, crushed
- Frozen whipped topping

Directions

1. Mix marked (▸) ingredients in large BlenderBottle® until well blended and pour into pie shell. Refrigerate 1 hour.
2. Top with a layer of whipped topping and crushed candy bars.

Tip: *Tastes great with toffee bars!*

Nutritional Information

(per serving: 366 cal., 13.6 g total fat (5.9 g sat. fat), 9 mg chol., 620 mg sodium, 57 g carbo., 48 g sugars, 4.7 g protein)

Key Lime Pie

Prep Time	**Chill Time**	**Servings**
10 minutes	2 Hours	8

Ingredients

- 1 (10-inch) graham cracker pie crust
- ▸ 1 c fresh lime juice
- ▸ 1 (14 oz.) can sweetened condensed milk
- ▸ 1 T grated lime zest
- ▸ 1 (3.5 oz.) package instant vanilla pudding mix
- 1 (8 oz.) tub frozen whipped topping, thawed

Directions

1. In a large BlenderBottle®, mix marked (▸) ingredients until smooth. Pour mixture into pie crust.
2. Gently fold in whipped topping until evenly mixed. Chill at least 2 hours.

Before serving, garnish with additional whipped topping and lime zest.

Tip: *Fresh lime juice makes this recipe a real winner!*

Nutritional Information

(per serving: 435 cal., 18.2 g total fat (8.2 g sat. fat), 38 mg chol., 450 mg sodium, 64 g carbo., 52.8 g sugars, 6.2 g protein)

Old Fashioned Buttermilk Pie

Prep Time	Cook Time	Servings
10 minutes	30-50 minutes cooking	8

Ingredients

1 unbaked 9-inch deep-dish pie crust
- ▸ 4 large eggs
- ▸ 1 c buttermilk
- ▸ 1/2 c butter, melted
- ▸ 1 t vanilla
- ▸ 2 T flour
- ▸ 1 pinch salt
- ▸ 1 1/4 c sugar

1-2 c frozen berries, thawed
2 c whipped cream

Directions

1. Preheat oven to 350° F (180° C).
2. In large BlenderBottle®, combine marked (▸) ingredients and mix well. Pour filling into uncooked pie shell.
3. Bake in preheated oven until the top is lightly browned and the center sets (about 50 minutes). Remove from oven and cool to room temperature. Top with berries and whipped cream.

Nutritional Information

(per serving: 523 cal., 31 g total fat (15.6 g sat. fat), 171 mg chol., 349 mg sodium, 57 g carbo., 45.8 g sugars, 6.4 g protein)

Simply the Best Pumpkin Pie

Prep Time	Cook Time	Servings
10 minutes	60 minutes	8

Ingredients

1 unbaked 9-inch deep-dish pie crust
1 3/4 c (15 oz. can) pumpkin
1 1/2 c (12 fluid oz. can) evaporated milk
- ▸ 2 large eggs
- ▸ 3/4 c granulated sugar
- ▸ 1 t ground cinnamon
- ▸ 1/2 t salt
- ▸ 1/2 t ground ginger
- ▸ 1/4 t ground cloves

Directions

1. Preheat oven to 425° F (220° C).
2. Combine marked (▸) ingredients in a large BlenderBottle® and blend until smooth.
3. Place pumpkin in large bowl and gradually stir in BlenderBottle mixture. Pour into pie shell.
4. Bake for 15 minutes. Reduce temperature to 350° F (180° C); bake for 40 to 50 minutes or until knife inserted near center comes out clean. Cool for 2 hours.

Nutritional Information

(per serving: 321 cal., 12.4 g total fat (4 g sat. fat), 67 mg chol., 388 mg sodium, 48 g carbo., 36 g sugars, 7 g protein)

Dark Chocolate Temptation Trifle

Prep Time
45 minutes

Servings
8

Ingredients

- 1 9x13 pan of brownies (prepared from mix)
- ▸ 1 (5.9 oz.) package instant chocolate pudding mix
- ▸ 3 c milk
- 1 16 oz. container frozen whipped topping, thawed
- 10 chocolate sandwich cookies, crushed

Directions

1. Line bottom of a large serving bowl with half of brownies.
2. Mix marked (▸) ingredients in a large BlenderBottle® and pour half over brownies in bowl.
3. Cover pudding with half of the whipped topping. Repeat layers.
4. Sprinkle top with crushed cookies and chill before serving.

Nutritional Information
(per serving: 545 cal., 11.2 g total fat (10 g sat. fat), 50 mg chol., 602.4 mg sodium, 42.5 g carbo., 63 g sugars, 6.6 g protein)

Simply Strawberry Trifle

Prep Time	Chill Time	Servings
20 minutes	2 hours	8

Ingredients

- ▸ 1 c cold milk
- ▸ 1 c (8 oz.) sour cream
- ▸ 1 package (3.4 oz.) instant vanilla pudding mix
- ▸ 1 t grated orange peel (optional)
- 1 (12 oz.) container frozen whipped topping, thawed
- 8 c cubed angel food cake
- 4 c sliced fresh strawberries

Directions

1. In a large BlenderBottle®, mix marked (▸) ingredients until smooth. Place half of the cake cubes in a 3-quart glass bowl. Arrange a third of the strawberries around sides of bowl and over cake; spoon half of pudding mixture on top of berries. Top with half of the whipped topping. Repeat layers once. Top with remaining berries and refrigerate for 2 hours before serving.

Tip: *Add bananas or additional berries for variety.*

Nutritional Information

(per serving: 364 cal., 16.7 g total fat (10.1 g sat. fat), 47 mg chol., 576 mg sodium, 49.3 g carbo., 19.7 g sugars, 6.3 g protein)

Custom-Colored Sugar

Prep Time
2 minutes

Makes Approximately
1 cup

Ingredients

- 1 c white sugar
- 2+ drops any color liquid food coloring

Directions

1. Add sugar to a small BlenderBottle® and place drops of food coloring in center. Shake until sugar is evenly colored. For deeper colors, add additional coloring and repeat until sugar reaches desired color.

Powdered Sugar Drizzle

Prep Time
5 minutes

Makes Approximately
1 cup

Ingredients

- 1/4 t vanilla extract
- 2 T milk or orange juice
- 1 c powdered sugar
- Extra milk as needed

Directions

1. Combine marked (▸) ingredients in a small BlenderBottle® and mix until smooth. Add extra milk, if needed, until mixture reaches drizzling consistency.

Chocolate Powdered Sugar Drizzle:
Prepare as above except use milk, not orange juice, and add 2 T unsweetened cocoa powder.

Nutritional Information
(per 1/8 cup serving: 61 cal., 0 g total fat (0 g sat. fat), 0 mg chol., 2 mg sodium, 15.1 g carbo., 15 g sugars, 0.1 g protein)

Measurements & Weights

CUPS

1/8 cup	=	30 mL
1/4 cup	=	60 mL
1/3 cup	=	80 mL
1/2 cup	=	120 mL
2/3 cup	=	160 mL
3/4 cup	=	180 mL
1 cup	=	240 mL
1-1/4 cups	=	300 mL
1-1/3 cups	=	320 mL
1-1/2 cups	=	360 mL
1-2/3 cups	=	400 mL
1-3/4 cups	=	420 mL
2 cups	=	480 mL
2-1/4 cups	=	540 mL
2-1/2 cups	=	600 mL
3 cups	=	720 mL

TEASPOOONS & TABLESPOONS

1/8 teaspoon	=	1 mL / 1.035 grams
1/4 teaspoon	=	2 mL / 2.07 grams
1/2 teaspoon	=	3 mL / 3.11 grams
3/4 teaspoon	=	4 mL / 4.14 grams
1 teaspoon	=	5 mL / 5.175 grams
1 1-1/4 teaspoons	=	7 mL / 7.25 grams
1-1/2 teaspoons	=	8 mL / 8.28 grams
2 teaspoons	=	10 mL / 10.35 grams
1 tablespoon	=	15 mL / 15.53 grams
1-1/2 tablespoons	=	23 mL / 23.81 grams
2 tablespoons	=	30 mL / 31.05 grams

TEASPOOONS & TABLESPOONS (Continued)

2-1/2 tablespoons	=	38 mL / 39.33 grams
3 tablespoons	=	45 mL / 46.58 grams
3-1/2 tablespoons	=	53 mL / 54.86 grams
16 tablespoons	=	1 cup
1 tablespoon	=	3 teaspoons

OUNCES

1 ounce / 2 tablespoons	=	30 mL / 31.05 grams
1 pint / 16 fluid ounces	=	453.6 grams (1 lb.)
28 fluid ounces	=	828 mL

DRY MEASURE

1 ounce	=	28.35 grams
1 pound / 16 ounces	=	453.6 grams
2.2 pounds	=	1 kilogram
1.035 mL	=	1 gram

ABBREVIATIONS

t	=	teaspoon
T	=	tablespoon
c	=	cup
oz.	=	ounce
lb.	=	pound
mL	=	milliliter

Common Ingredient Substitutions

If you don't have one of the ingredients for a recipe, try one of these quick substitutions!

Ingredient	Amount	Substitution
Baking powder	1 teaspoon	1/4 t baking soda plus 1/2 t cream of tartar OR 1/4 t baking soda plus 1/2 c buttermilk (decrease liquid in recipe by 1/2 c)
Broth: beef or chicken	1 cup	1 T soy sauce plus enough water to make 1 c OR 1 c vegetable broth
Brown sugar	1 cup, packed	1 c white sugar plus 1/4 c molasses and decrease the liquid in recipe by 1/4 c OR 1 1/4 c confectioners' sugar OR 1 c white sugar
Buttermilk	1 cup	1 T lemon juice or vinegar plus enough milk to make 1 c OR 1 c yogurt
Corn syrup	1 cup	1 1/4 c white sugar plus 1/3 c water OR 1 c honey
Cream (half and half)	1 cup	7/8 c milk plus 1 T butter
Cream (heavy)	1 cup	1 c evaporated milk OR 3/4 c milk plus 1/3 c butter
Cream (light)	1 cup	1 c evaporated milk OR 3/4 c milk plus 3 T butter
Garlic	1 clove	1/8 t garlic powder OR 1/2 t granulated garlic OR 1/2 t garlic salt--reduce salt in recipe
Hot pepper sauce	1 teaspoon	3/4 t cayenne pepper plus 1 t vinegar
Mayonnaise	1 cup	1 c plain yogurt OR 1 c sour cream
Molasses	1 cup	3/4 c brown sugar and 1 t cream of tartar
Sour cream	1 cup	1 c plain yogurt OR 1 T lemon juice or vinegar mixed with enough cream to make 1 c OR 3/4 c buttermilk mixed with 1/3 c butter
Soy sauce	1/2 cup	4 T Worcestershire sauce mixed with 1 T water
Vinegar	1 teaspoon	1 t lemon or lime juice OR 2 t white wine
White sugar	1 cup	1 1/4 c confectioners' sugar OR 1 c brown sugar OR 3/4 c honey OR 3/4 c corn syrup
Yogurt	1 cup	1 c buttermilk OR 1 c sour cream OR 1 c sour milk
Chocolate Protein Powder	1 serving	1 serving vanilla protein powder plus 1 T cocoa powder

Index

(GF) **Gluten-Free** – *Recipe is gluten-free*
(M) **Gluten-Free when Modified** – *Recipe can be made gluten-free by using gluten-free soy sauce, dressing mixes, etc.*